THIS IS ADHD

A WORKBOOK

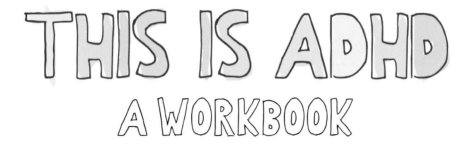

THIS IS ADHD
A WORKBOOK

Practical Advice and Interactive Journaling for Understanding ADHD

Chanelle Moriah
Best-selling author of *I Am Autistic*

Published in the United States by:
Ulysses Press
PO Box 3440
Berkeley, CA 94703
www.ulyssespress.com

First published in 2023 as THIS IS ADHD in Australia and New Zealand by Allen & Unwin

ISBN: 978-1-64604-612-6

Design by Chanelle Moriah and Megan van Staden
Fonts by Chanelle Moriah
Author photo by Judah Plester

Printed in China
2 4 6 8 10 9 7 5 3 1

This book belongs to

_____

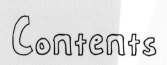

Contents

How to use this book 10

Language 11

What is ADHD? 12

Types of ADHD 13

Summary of ADHD traits 14

Fidgeting and restlessness 16

Body-focused repetitive behaviors 17

Interrupting people 18

Managing interruptions 20

Volume control 21

Talking fast 22

"Excessive" talking 24

Forgetfulness 26

Managing forgetfulness 28

Losing train of thought 32

Object permanence 34

Misplacing belongings 36

Forgetting to eat and drink 37

Concentration and distractibility 38

Staying on task 40

Hyper-focus / hyper-fixation 42

Perseveration 44

Zoning out or dissociating 45

Attention to detail 46

Impulsivity 48

Danger 50

Crisis and emergency 51

Difficulties summarized 52

Positives 53

Time agnosia vs. time blindness 54

Time agnosia 55

Managing time agnosia 56

Relationships 58

Masking 60

Rejection Sensitive Dysphoria (RSD) 64

Self-esteem 66

Criticism 67

Emotional dysregulation 68

Mood swings 69

Reactivity and sensitivity 70

Empathy 72

Depression 74

Anxiety.. 76

Burnout / overload.. 78

Sleep disturbance.. 80

Suggestions to improve sleep 81

Executive dysfunction 82

Trouble with making or sticking to routines...................... 85

Disorganization... 86

Body doubling 87

ADHD paralysis 88

Laziness... 90

Waiting mode 92

Being told what to do 94

Dopamine... 96

Ways to get dopamine... 97

Interest-based vs. importance-based nervous system........... 98

Boredom... 100

Reward systems.. 104

Trouble finishing projects or tasks...................................... 106

Spontaneity.. 108

Sugar.. 109

Addiction.. 110

Stimulation 111

Sensory overload.. 112

Clumsiness... 114

Proprioception... 115

Vestibular system.. 116

Interoception.. 117

Listening... 118

Learning styles 122

Reading... 124

Medication.. 126

Medication side effects... 127

My experience with medication... 128

Caffeine.. 130

Presentation and age 131

Myths... 132

Importance of accommodations / adjustments..................... 134

Reframing traits.. 136

Acknowledgments... 138

About the author 140

How to use this book

The first priority is that you use this book in whatever way is the most useful to you.

But if you'd like some structure, here is my intention and a key to explain the different components.

This book is designed to help you learn about yourself, whether you are formally or self-diagnosed with ADHD, or if you are questioning whether you might have it. It is also designed to help others understand why you do certain things.

☐ — Use these boxes to mark off the things that relate to your experience.

And that's it, really. Super simple!
I hope this book helps you to learn about yourself, and becomes a useful tool to share with others.

Use these boxes to write, draw, or scribble your own thoughts, feelings, or experiences.

Language

Those who are immersed in the disabled, neurodivergent, or autistic communities may have come across the concept of identity-first language versus person-first language. Identity-first language uses terms like "autistic," "d/Deaf," "blind," "disabled," etc., while person-first language uses terms like "person with autism" or "person with a disability."

I am autistic with ADHD. I cannot speak to the preferences of other disabled communities, but the majority of autistic individuals prefer identity-first language. When it comes to ADHD, language can be a bit more of a gray area, because there isn't really a word for ADHD individuals — not yet, anyway. Some may refer to themselves as an ADHDer or AuDHD (if, like me, they are also autistic). Others may say "I am ADHD" or "I have ADHD."

As with anything (gender, name, disability, pronouns, etc.), it is important to respect the preferences of individuals and how they wish to be referred to. For the purposes of this book, since I am speaking to and about an entire community, I will use a combination of language types.

What is ADHD?

ADHD stands for Attention Deficit / Hyperactivity Disorder.

It is a neurodevelopmental condition, which means it relates to, or involves, the development of a person's nervous system.

Essentially, the nervous system is the communicator between our body and our brain. It controls our motor functions (movement), senses, thought processes, and awareness, and plays a part in our learning and memory. It is also responsible for regulating our internal physical state, such as our body temperature.

ADHD is a condition in which our nervous system has developed differently and functions differently to that of most people. It involves all aspects of how our minds and bodies work.

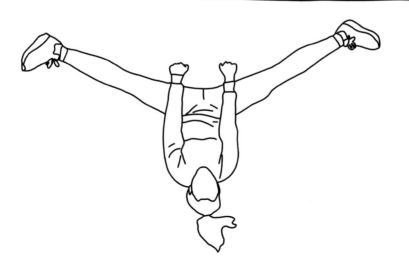

Types of ADHD

There are three recognized types of ADHD: impulsive / hyperactive, inattentive, and combined. However, as someone who is not a professional, it is difficult for me to find a clear-cut way to split up and categorize each of the traits and experiences that I will cover in this book. Every individual will have a different presentation and trait combination, so I won't be dividing this book into categories. Besides, our understanding of neurodevelopmental conditions is constantly changing and growing. The diagnostic terms around ADHD have already changed a few times. Who knows what they will look like in the future, as we expand our knowledge.

Instead, I will explain some of the many traits of ADHDers to give a starting point for further understanding.

Summary of ADHD traits

☐ Emotional dysregulation (see page 68)

☐ Disorganization (see page 86)

☐ Zoning out (see page 45)

☐ Distractibility (see page 38)

☐ Lack of attention to detail (see page 46)

☐ Creativity

☐ Impatience

☐ Forgetfulness (see page 26)

☐ Executive dysfunction (see page 82)

Restlessness / inability to sit still (see page 16)

Fidgeting (see page 16)

Talkativeness (see page 24)

Interrupting people (see page 18)

Time agnosia (see page 55)

Impulsivity (see page 48)

Reduced sense of danger (see page 50)

Hyper-focus (see page 42)

Fidgeting and restlessness

Fidgeting is a common trait of ADHD and is not dissimilar to the concept of stimming (a repetitive movement, action, or sound made for self-stimulation or emotional regulation). Stimming is something that everyone does, but it is seen more intensely in conditions such as autism and ADHD. Sometimes it's actions like tapping pens or jiggling legs, but it can present in many more ways, especially as people grow older and learn to adapt to their environment. In the case of ADHD, fidgeting can also be related to anxiety, hyperactivity, or dopamine seeking (see page 97).

Many of us with ADHD will have a hard time sitting still or focusing when we are required to.

Here are some ways that it might present:

- ☐ Biting nails
- ☐ Twirling hair
- ☐ Cracking knuckles
- ☐ Drumming fingers
- ☐ Tapping a pencil
- ☐ Bouncing legs
- ☐ Tapping feet
- ☐ Pacing
- ☐ Doodling
- ☐ Humming
- ☐ Scratching
- ☐ Rocking
- ☐ Chewing on pens or pencils
- ☐ Constantly changing positions

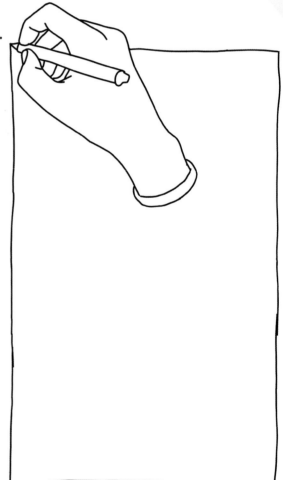

Body-focused repetitive behaviors

This is a trait that may be more commonly associated with Obsessive-Compulsive Disorder or anxiety-related tendencies, but there is a bit of crossover.

For some individuals with ADHD, the combination of fidgeting, restlessness, impulsivity (see page 48), hyper-fixation (see page 42), and stimulation seeking (see page 111) may result in some slightly harmful behaviors such as skin and scab picking, popping pimples, biting nails, grinding or clenching teeth, and pulling or plucking body hairs.

Some people may also find that they become fixated and lose track of time while doing so.

Interrupting people

It is not uncommon for people with ADHD to interrupt conversation or finish other people's sentences. There are a few reasons this might happen:

The impulse or urge to speak makes it harder to wait my turn to say what I want to say.

It is difficult to wait through what another person is saying when I already know where the conversation is going.

I am afraid that I might forget what I want to say.

I am afraid the conversation will move on before I get a chance to say something.

The longer the conversation goes on, the more thoughts I have and the harder it becomes to keep them all in order for when I get a chance to talk.

I am struggling to stay focused.

I am not trying to be rude when I interrupt you. I want to hear what you're saying, but sometimes the effort of holding on to my thoughts, trying to stop myself from acting on impulse, finding an appropriate gap in which to start talking, and keeping myself focused means that I am unable to actively listen. Trying to manage all of this at once can be quite overwhelming.

Individuals with ADHD will often be aware that interrupting people will be perceived as rude or disrespectful, and they will often feel bad about doing it. This can also have a significant impact on their mental health.

The increase in virtual meetings over the past few years has made things even more difficult. On screen, it is harder to tell when there is an appropriate gap in which to speak and there is a higher chance of interrupting someone, especially when you take internet speed and technical issues into account.

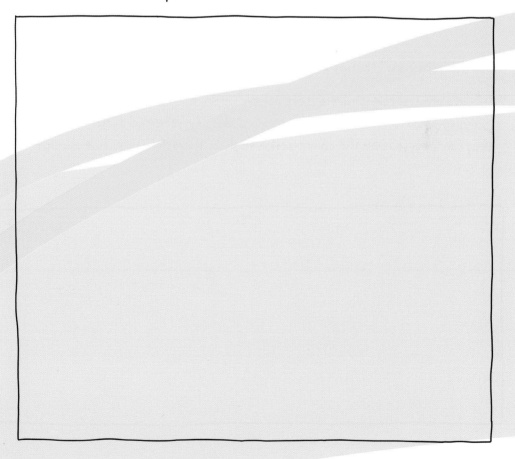

Managing interruptions

Here are some possible strategies to manage interrupting others:

* Write down your thoughts or the things you want to say, or put them in a note on your phone. If you are meeting in person, the other people need to understand that they aren't being ignored when you do this — it's easier if you are meeting virtually.

* When you interrupt someone, acknowledge it, apologize, and bring the conversation back to what they were saying. This way you are showing them that you value their voice.

* Use a gesture to indicate that you have something you want to say. For example, raising your hand, putting your finger on your cheek or nose, putting your hand on your shoulder — it can be anything. Make it fun or subtle; it's up to you. But make sure everyone understands the meaning of whatever gesture you choose.

* Use the "raise hand" feature in virtual meetings to signal that you have something to say.

* In a group setting, have a "safe person" — someone you can quietly share your thoughts with. That way there's someone else who remembers your thoughts, and they can bring you into the conversation to share them if that's what you want to do.

Volume control

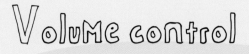

Some individuals with ADHD have a hard time regulating the volume at which they speak. They may be inclined to speak louder than necessary without being aware of it. If it is pointed out, they might quiet down at first but slowly return to their original volume.

Many people with ADHD are often more energetic or passionate than their neurotypical peers, and this can come out in the form of increased speaking volume. We often have very busy minds, and for some of us it feels like we have to talk over our own thoughts to keep ourselves on track. Unfortunately, when people point out this behavior, it can often result in the individual feeling shut down or not accepted for who they are.

Talking Fast

ADHD individuals can be known to talk quite fast. There are probably a few reasons for this. One is that it is a presentation of the hyperactivity associated with ADHD. Another is that the ADHD brain often runs faster than we can keep up with. Talking fast gives us a higher chance of getting the thought out before it vanishes into a crowd of other thoughts.

Fast talking might also be related to the extremes at which an ADHD individual can experience emotion. It makes sense that we might speak quite fast when we are very passionate, excited, or distressed about something.

Regardless of the reason, a lot of the time the ADHD individual isn't even aware that they are speaking faster than anyone else. However, pointing it out may not be helpful. It will likely make us focus on the speed we are talking at, which makes us more likely to forget what we are trying to say.

In line with this, ADHD individuals can find it difficult to stay focused when things are moving too slowly. This can actually become quite frustrating. This is one way in which online learning can benefit some people with ADHD — they might be able to speed up the recording, which can make it easier to keep up and stay engaged. Online study also gives them the freedom to choose the most effective time and way to engage in the learning.

"Excessive" talking

Many people with ADHD do talk quite a lot. It is a more subtle way for the hyperactive element of ADHD to present itself, and often goes undetected. The ADHD brain is often very busy and this can result in us having a lot to say, especially when combined with impulsivity (see page 48). It can be incredibly difficult to keep chatter short and to the point when your brain is firing off on a number of different thought paths, moving way faster than your thoughts can be organized.

Talking a lot or using extra words can also act as a mask when we forget what we are talking about, which is common with ADHD. On top of that, silence can be something that is difficult to sit with, so talking fills that space.

However, labeling our talking as "excessive" implies that this is a negative trait, which can play into Rejection Sensitive Dysphoria (see page 64). It takes an element of who the person is, how they express emotion, or how they communicate — and something they often can't help — and turns it into an annoyance. It puts some ADHDers in a place where we feel that we are not free to contribute to a conversation, because doing so results in a reminder that we aren't acting "correctly" or leads to us feeling like a burden.

We aren't trying to be annoying or take up too much time — we're simply communicating based on the way that our brain works. Spending all day every day trying to act and communicate in a neurotypical way can be extremely exhausting, self-sacrificing, and sometimes impossible. It should be seen as a good thing when the ADHD individual talks freely, without suddenly withdrawing, because it can mean that we are comfortable enough to be the authentic version of ourselves.

If the amount of talking we do makes you feel unheard, have a conversation about that. Explain what we can do to make you feel heard. In what ways can we freely be ourselves and be heard, but still ensure that you feel valued? It is a team effort, and space should be allowed for both parties.

If you are an ADHDer, remember: you are not too much, too present, too big, or too talkative. You are valuable and just as worthy of space as anyone else. Don't minimize yourself and your worth.

Forgetfulness

There are a number of ways in which ADHD individuals might experience forgetfulness.

For example, I might:

☐ Forget what I am talking about

☐ Forget something I wanted to say or do

☐ Struggle with object permanence (see page 34)

☐ Lose objects or belongings

☐ Miss appointments or commitments

☐ Forget what I need to get when I go shopping

☐ Forget to bring something with me when I go out or when I am preparing to do an activity

Forgetfulness, when associated with ADHD, is quite interesting. You might think it suggests that the person has a bad memory, but this is often not the case. ADHDers typically do not have difficulties with long-term memory. We can store and collect plenty of information, which can contribute to the busyness of an ADHD brain. Do I need to remember a poem I read ten years ago? No! Does my brain insist on replaying it randomly every few months? Yes!

ADHD individuals will often have difficulties with short-term or working memory. This means that our brains seem to delete information that we need in the immediate future, often choosing to focus on something completely irrelevant instead (unless we are hyper-focused or particularly interested in something).

Managing Forgetfulness

Here are some tools that might be useful for managing forgetfulness. Keep in mind that every person is different, and any strategy may not work 100 percent of the time.

- Have a to-do list on the fridge or in your room, and add to it whenever you think of a task that needs doing. But don't expect yourself to get an unreasonable number of things done on any given day — the to-do list is just to help you avoid forgetting the task.

- Use a digital calendar or scheduling app that sends reminders and notifications. This also works with voice assistants such as Alexa or Google Home.

- Print out visual lists of things you need for different activities. Check that you've got all of the items before you go out.

- Leave visual reminders in inconvenient places — laundry on the bed, or the vacuum cleaner in the middle of the floor. You still may not get the task done, but you'll be more likely to remember it needs doing.

- Set timers when you're cooking.

- Write things down — even if they seem silly or simple in the moment. Write it down.

- Unpack your bag immediately when you get home.

Here are a few other things that I try to do to manage my forgetfulness.
They don't always work, but they can sometimes be useful.

Counting off essential items

I have six items that I take with me whenever I leave the house: my phone, wallet, keys, sunflower lanyard, headphones, and watch. Every time I leave the house, I count all six items. If my watch battery has run out and needs to be charged, it still needs to be accounted for. I have to know where all six items are before I leave the house.

I've just made it a habit. Before I open the front door, I count the six items out loud while either touching or looking at them, and then I can go. If I am going to cheerleading, I need to count six items plus my shoes, water bottle, and a snack.

Using numbers to count off the essential six items means I have fewer things to think about when I'm going to activities and need to take additional things. This means I'm less likely to leave something behind. It's not fool-proof, but I find it helps. (Please do note that I am writing this as someone who is also autistic. Many ADHDers find it difficult or impossible to create and form habits.)

Using Tiimo

Tiimo is an app designed with neurodivergent people in mind. It allows you to create a routine with emojis and pictures as well as text. Within the routine, I also make checklists, and each item can have an associated picture. For example, I plan a time to pack my bag, then under that task I have the list of items that I need to pack, with pictures beside them. This makes it easier to check that I've got them all.

Scheduling extra time

When I schedule appointments, I also schedule travel and "get ready" time, and break that into tasks such as packing my bag, getting dressed, etc. I still sometimes forget to do this, but when I do remember it is super helpful.

Losing train of thought

For a person with ADHD, it can be really common to forget what you're talking about in the middle of what you're saying, or to forget what you're supposed to be doing while you're doing it. I'll talk more about this second point in the sections on object permanence (see page 34) and executive dysfunction (see page 82).

As I've said previously, the ADHD brain runs so fast and there's so much going on in our minds at any given point that it's really easy to lose our grip on the information we need right at that moment. Personally, if I'm answering a question and I forget what the question was partway through, I will just stop and quite bluntly say that I've forgotten the question. Some people might try to mask the fact that they've forgotten, and they might stall while they search their thoughts for the original topic. Others might find that they just go completely blank — it's like "you can have all of these irrelevant thoughts or none at all."

It's honestly quite a frustrating experience — sometimes I can actually feel the thought slipping away and there's nothing I can do about it. If I go to quickly write it down, my brain will start thinking about writing and forget what I wanted to write. The saying "I can't hear myself think" can be somewhat literal for an ADHD individual!

Losing track of what you're saying can also be quite anxiety-provoking or cause feelings of embarrassment. It can also play into Rejection Sensitive Dysphoria (see page 64), as you find yourself frantically trying to figure out what you were saying while others are waiting.

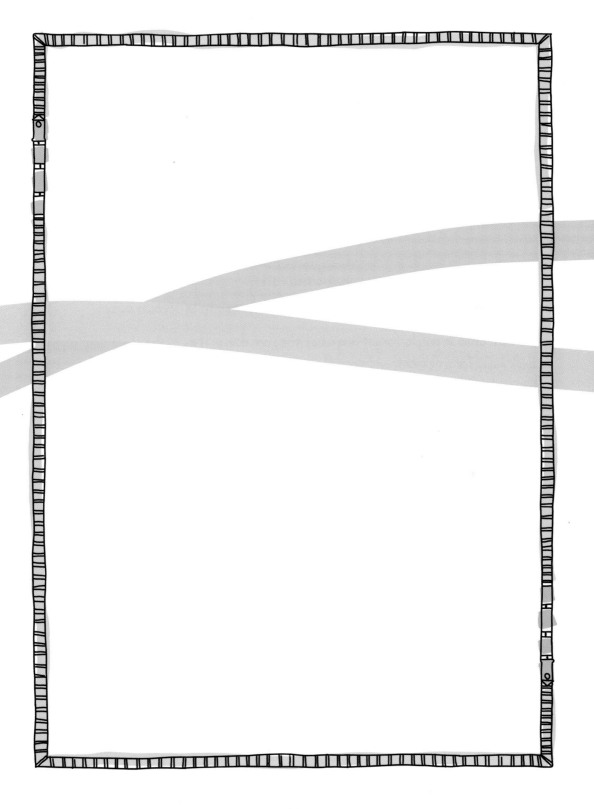

Object perManence

Some ADHD individuals may experience a degree of lack of object permanence. This is your ability to remember things that you cannot see. I am not referring to object permanence in the same way that an infant is not aware that things they cannot see still exist, but it is similar in the sense that if you cannot see something, you might forget about it entirely.

Essentially this can be summarized as "out of sight, out of mind." For example, if you cannot see the leftovers in the back of the fridge, you might forget that they exist until it is too late to eat them and they need to be thrown away.

This can result in people forgetting what they are doing. They might start cooking but walk away for a moment, and since they cannot see the stove, they forget about it. They might forget to do homework because it comes home in their bag and they cannot see it in order to remember to get it done.

To manage this, a neurodivergent person might organize their belongings in such a way that all or most items are regularly visible. This may seem messy and disorganized to everyone else, but it's best left alone. (Unless it is a safety hazard… obviously.) We can find it really overwhelming if someone else moves or cleans up our items, because once we can't see it, we may have a hard time remembering what we are even looking for.

This is also one reason why we may not take the initiative when it comes to tasks that involve other people's belongings. I don't want you to move my things, so I won't move yours — unless you ask me to, and you tell me where everything goes.

Unfortunately, this lack of object permanence sometimes carries over to things like text messages or even people. It sounds awful, but sometimes the ADHD brain can seemingly forget other people. The ADHD individual may have every intention of messaging or checking in with their friend, but may find that they don't follow through because they remember at inappropriate or inconvenient times. Then, when there is an appropriate time, there's no visual reminder of that person's existence. If the ADHDer opens a text or message and plans to respond later, it's a lot easier to forget about it once there's no active notification.

Misplacing belongings

This is another topic that involves a number of ADHD traits. It's related to executive functioning (see page 82), object permanence (see page 34), distractibility (see page 38), forgetfulness (see page 26), and even zoning out (see page 45). If an ADHDer does not have a set location where they keep or put things, it is very easy to misplace belongings.

As I've explained, some ADHDers will appear messy or disorganized because they leave items in view as a way of coping with their difficulty with object permanence. So, in many situations, they already have a lot to look at. Then, if the ADHD individual walks off with an item and gets distracted by another task (related to both distractibility and executive dysfunction), they may put that item down where they are and pick up something else.

This can happen over and over again, so what you end up with is a series of objects left in the wrong place. Add in forgetfulness and it's the perfect combination for an unwanted treasure hunt ... several times a day ... every day. On top of this, it can happen while the individual is zoned out or daydreaming, which will make it even harder to recall where the item might have been placed. This can even mean "losing" objects you placed in your pocket just moments ago. Out of sight, out of mind, right?

On the flip side of this, while some ADHDers may easily misplace or lose things, they may also have an incredible ability to recall very specific locations of very specific items. For example, a blue pen that is in between the first and second cushions on the left side of the couch in the living room, or a battery that's sitting by a jewelry box on the bedside table in the spare bedroom.

Forgetting to eat and drink

There are a number of reasons why ADHDers might forget to eat or drink. A large contributor to forgetting to eat is simply distraction. We may have intended to grab something to eat but wound up doing something else, or we may be too hyper-focused on a task or activity to be able to walk away even for a moment. It's also really easy to put down a glass of water and forget it exists, at the same time thinking that you had a drink because you remember going to get it.

Another element at play when it comes to forgetting to eat or drink is executive dysfunction (see page 82). It can take a lot of steps and focus to put together a meal or get a drink, and this can reduce motivation, which further reduces the chances of us remembering to do it, especially if there's something more interesting to think about. It becomes kind of a chore, especially for individuals who also have poor interoception (see page 117), which is particularly common among those who are also autistic.

Solutions or suggestions:

* Set alarms or reminders for times to eat or drink.

* Get a large bottle, fill it up once in the morning, and aim to drink it all by the end of the day. This provides a visual reminder of how much you've actually had to drink.

* Allow grazing foods or snacks, rather than insisting on regular meals.

Forgetting to eat can also lead to unhealthy eating patterns — for example, ADHD individuals might go all day forgetting to sustain themselves, then when they finally realize they need to eat, they are extra hungry, so they consume excessive amounts of food all at once.

Concentration and distractibility

Many ADHD individuals will find that they have a hard time focusing. There are a number of reasons for this, but many are connected to the low levels of dopamine associated with ADHD (see page 96). Difficulty concentrating or being easily distracted can also be put down to executive dysfunction (see page 82), having a busy brain, or not being interested in the thing that needs focus in that moment.

For ADHDers, there's so much going on in our minds, and our brains don't seem to be particularly good at filtering out the unimportant information or being able to highlight and hold on to what is needed at that moment. This can result in us getting distracted, forgetting we're speaking, or stopping mid-sentence.

Think of it like this:

In a neurotypical brain, you might have a file box of thoughts, and you can pick out the ones you need when you need them. Sure, you might pick out some unnecessary ones sometimes, but for the most part it's under control and you can usually put them away when they're not needed.

With an ADHD brain, there are no files, just a huge number of thoughts and memories flying around randomly.

The brain is like, "Oooh, look at that one!"

"Oh, and this one too!"

"What's that? Oh, a song."

"Oops, I dropped one. I don't know which one it was. Oh well."

"Hey, remember this thing?"

"Look at this one ..."

Staying on task

In line with having trouble focusing, staying on task — particularly when working on something we find boring — can be very difficult. Again, this is related to other topics such as dopamine (see page 96) and executive dysfunction (see page 82).

Staying on task requires the management of a lot of things. The ADHD individual often has to deal with their brain going off on a number of different tangents, thinking of some random fact they learned several years ago, having one line of a song replay in their mind over and over, and avoiding perseveration (see page 44) for something that is not immediately important. They also have to manage and avoid environmental distractions or interruptions, while still ensuring there's enough stimulation to reduce the chances of getting too bored. Some individuals might find that it's just impossible to stick to one task, and will frequently change what they are doing.

One strategy I use to work with my brain on this is to make a list of things that I need to do (keeping it to an achievable length), then cycle through it, doing ten minutes of each thing before moving on to the next. Once I reach the end of the list, I go back to the start and repeat this process until I've crossed everything off. I don't always stick strictly to the ten minutes, though. If I'm ten minutes into a task and I'm finding that I'm not distracted and could quite easily keep going, I'll do that task until my brain has had enough.

Hyper-focus / hyper-fixation

On the flip side of having difficulty with concentration, if the ADHD brain picks up something particularly interesting, it might filter out everything but that thing. We can completely lose track of time or the need to eat, sleep, go to the toilet, or be somewhere else. We may not notice or process the fact that someone is speaking to us. This may go on for several hours. It can be incredibly difficult to walk away from what we are doing, even if we realize that it's late or we have another commitment to get to.

This trait can be really positive, but it can also be quite debilitating or counterproductive. You can get a lot done when you are completely oblivious to literally everything else, but when you add in executive dysfunction (see page 82) it can end up being quite a mess.

For example, we might wake up one day and find ourselves hyper-focused on cleaning. That sounds great, right? Sure! But then cleaning the room turns into rearranging the whole house, while simultaneously deep-cleaning the grout between the tiles, reorganizing the Tupperware drawer, and repairing a broken table leg. Next thing you know, you're repainting the walls. It's not a matter of finishing one task and then starting another. You start them all and probably only finish one or two, if any.

But, like I said, it can be a really positive trait. I can write and illustrate an entire book in six weeks when I'm hyper-focused. I've also gone out and bought a sewing machine, taught myself to sew without any previous experience, and made a perfectly fitting skater dress with pockets, zippers, and an elasticized waistband — all without a pattern, and I did it in less than a day. Have I used that skill ever again? No, absolutely not, but my brain was determined to do it that day.

Perseveration

Perseveration is similar to hyper-focus. It's the concept of being stuck on a thought, feeling, or action. Perseveration is a trait that some people will associate with autism, but some ADHDers experience it as well.

It can often prevent us from doing or thinking about anything else. For example, I might be trying to sleep, but my brain is stuck thinking about an email I need to send and how I will word it. If I get up and send that email, then I'll be able to go to sleep.

Others will find that even after tending to the task or responding to the thought, they will still be stuck thinking about it. Sometimes it isn't something that can be dealt with immediately, but they still won't be able to put it aside. It can be very frustrating and, frankly, disabling.

Another example for me is that if someone says or does something that is hurtful and I can't make sense of the "why" behind it, I'll be stuck feeling hurt and angry and will not be able to move on or focus on anything else until I can understand the cause or logic behind the action.

Zoning out or dissociating

** Please note: I am not referring here to dissociative disorders. If you experience dissociation, you should seek a professional opinion about what might be causing it.

"Zoning out" is similar to daydreaming or losing focus. You may not be particularly aware of your surroundings or you may not notice someone trying to get your attention. However, it is usually fairly easy to snap out of.

Dissociating is more severe. It is often described as feeling a disconnection between your body and your mind. It can feel like you have no control over your body — as if you are in the passenger seat. It can also impact your memory and make you feel disoriented.

Both can affect your perception of time. Zoning out and dissociating can also be connected with overstimulation, and may then lead to shutting down.

Do you experience this? What happens? What does it feel like? When does it happen?

Attention to detail

Many people with ADHD will have trouble with attention to detail. This is partly because looking at smaller components requires greater focus. Paying attention to detail also often means there are a lot more steps or aspects to a task to think about. These can be difficult to keep organized in your mind if you struggle with executive dysfunction (see page 82). It can also be quite overwhelming trying to focus on several smaller things, as opposed to one big thing, when your brain is already very busy and not particularly good at filtering and holding on to information.

Another issue that comes with executive dysfunction is that it can be difficult to finish tasks. Often, looking through smaller details is a final step when you're trying to complete something, for example proofreading something you've written. ADHDers also struggle with their motivation being based on interest (see page 98). Reading over an assignment you've already written to check for spelling errors is boring and therefore even harder to focus on. There's little to spark interest and therefore motivation.

However, when we are particularly interested in something, we can become incredibly detail-focused and pick up things that others do not.

I'd also like to say here that just because some things are harder for ADHD people does not mean that those things are impossible or that they can't do them. Don't dismiss ADHDers as incapable, but cut them some slack when they make a mistake. It might be something silly that you think should have been easy to avoid, but for them it might take a lot more effort.

Impulsivity

To be impulsive is to do something without forethought or planning. It is usually a strong urge and often isn't a conscious decision. ADHD individuals aren't simply ignoring the consequences of their actions. It takes a lot of self-awareness and self-control to notice an impulse and choose not to act on it, particularly when you have a condition that is characterised by impulsivity.

Ways it may present:

Starting several tasks before finishing the previous ones (also related to distractibility and executive dysfunction)

Interrupting people

Saying things I might not mean to say

Binge eating

Going on a spontaneous vacation

Quitting a job, activity, or sport

Starting a new hobby that I'll probably only do once

Emotional outbursts

Oversharing

Spending money

Restarting (for example, I'm partway through a painting when I suddenly decide I hate it and start painting over it)

Impulsive behaviors such as spending, suddenly starting a new hobby, or taking a trip somewhere are also unfortunately really good sources of dopamine (see page 96). So doing something impulsively can feel really rewarding, even if only briefly. On top of that, living with a fast-paced brain often makes it difficult to do or manage things slowly — thinking things through takes extra time and requires at least some focus. Waiting is slow and boring and often feels unnecessary in the moment, especially when you have an irresistible or very strong urge to do something immediately.

Here's the thing, though: even when we are very self-aware and can think things through, it can still be incredibly difficult to choose not to act on the impulsive thoughts, regardless of the consequences. However, that doesn't mean that we have no self-control or can't learn to manage our impulses.

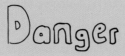

Danger

It is important to remember that not everyone is the same. Some people might experience the opposite of what I'm talking about here, but the following is a shared experience among some ADHD individuals.

ADHDers will sometimes have a reduced sense or awareness of danger. We may also be more inclined to participate in dangerous activities. We may be distracted, zoned out, or overwhelmed, and therefore not paying attention to our surroundings in order to notice hazards, or we may choose to engage in risky behaviors because doing so often increases dopamine levels (see page 96). Alternatively, we may just not be aware that something is dangerous. We may not fully think about it.

While this can, for obvious reasons, be a safety risk, it is also one of the reasons ADHDers are often fantastic in crisis or emergency situations.

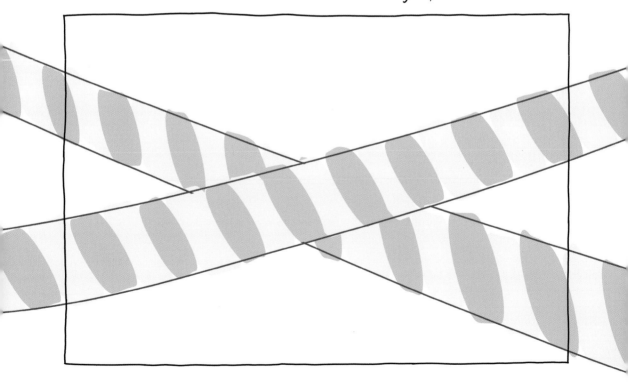

Crisis and emergency

ADHDers can often make really good responders in the event of an emergency.

The neurotransmitters adrenaline (also known as epinephrine) and norepinephrine both play a part in the body's natural fight-or-flight response. Both are stimulants. (As a side note, norepinephrine is one of the neurotransmitters that is targeted and increased by some ADHD medications because — for some individuals — it reduces certain challenges associated with ADHD, such as difficulty focusing.) So in a situation where a neurotypical person might be shaky, stressed, afraid, operating in survival mode, and struggling to process their thoughts, an ADHD person might be right in their element.

Having a reduced sense of danger means the ADHD individual is less likely to react out of fear. Increased amounts of stimulants pumping through the body make it easier to focus on what is needed while remaining calm, and being a fast thinker allows them to problem-solve quickly.

DIFFICULTIES
suMMarized

Masking (see page 60) ☐

☐ Executive dysfunction (see page 82)

☐ Sleep disturbance (see page 80)

ADHD paralysis (see page 88) ☐

☐ Time agnosia (see page 55)

☐ Emotional dysregulation (see page 68)

☐ Rejection Sensitive Dysphoria (see page 64)

☐ Disorganization (see page 86)

☐ Distractibility (see page 38)

Mental ☐ health issues

Positives

Here are some positive traits that may come with ADHD.

Note that everyone's experiences are different. If you don't relate to these, I encourage you to figure out what ADHD traits or experiences you have that are positive. ADHD shapes and impacts how you experience and go through life, so it is a significant part of who you are. Many ADHD individuals also have difficulties with self-esteem, so it is really important to consider, identify, and remember the many positive aspects that make you, you.

☐ Creative

☐ Arty and crafty

☐ Great in a crisis

☐ Fast thinker and learner

☐ Out-of-the-box thinker

☐ Loves trying new things

☐ Hyper-focused

☐ Adventurous

☐ Problem-solver

☐ Energetic

☐ Determined

☐ Funny

☐ Ambitious

☐ Empathetic

Time agnosia vs. time blindness

Before I get into this as a topic, let's talk about the language, and the difference between time agnosia and time blindness. By definition, agnosia refers to the "inability to interpret sensations" — in this case the inability to perceive the passing of time.

By definition, blindness refers to the state or condition of being unable to see or to a lack of perception, awareness, or judgment, or ignorance about something.

That last part is the important part to think about: "ignorance." We often use the term "blind" in a very negative way that suggests a person is deliberately choosing not to see or pay attention to a particular thing. In this way, for the blind community it would be similar to saying that "everyone is a little bit ADHD" or "someone is being a bit ADHD" when actually they are just distracted. It would be similar to calling someone a psycho or saying "you're a bit bipolar" just because you're having an emotional day. These are labels for conditions, and using them as adjectives is ignorant and ableist.

So, while "blindness" with regard to "time blindness" makes sense, given that sometimes ADHD individuals cannot perceive time, it is also a term that comes with a lot of negativity when used incorrectly. It has the potential to be harmful and hurtful to the blind community. I am not blind, so I am not in a position to say whether this term is offensive, but since some have verbalized that "time blindness" is an ableist term, I am using "time agnosia" instead.

Time agnosia

ADHDers commonly have difficulties with the perception of time and how much of it has passed. This can result in the individual consistently being either early or late (usually the latter), or missing commitments entirely. This is one reason (among many others) why it can be difficult for us ADHDers to stick to a routine. Even if we do have a plan, we frequently lose track of how much time we are taking to complete each task, and can ultimately fall behind regardless of how hard we try.

Another common experience for young ADHDers is that a parent or teacher will instruct us to do something and we'll agree to do it soon, or in the next few minutes, but then much more time can pass and the adult will get mad. We may or may not realize that more time has passed than we anticipated, but either way, we're now in trouble or being called lazy for something that often can't be managed without the right tools or support. This can also happen as a result of executive dysfunction (see page 82) or ADHD paralysis (see page 88).

For an ADHDer who is also autistic, time agnosia can be particularly distressing. Autistic individuals will often have a need for routine, and for things to be planned and be on time. When this doesn't happen, it can cause significant overwhelm.

Managing time agnosia

Here are some suggestions for how you might manage time agnosia:

☐ Set alarms.

☐ Use a scheduling app that sends notifications.

☐ Use a tool like Alexa to give you reminders. Setting verbal reminders reduces the chances of you getting distracted or losing the thought, as you might in the time it would take to find a device and open the appropriate app.

☐ If you are a parent or teacher, give the person ten-, five-, and two-minute warnings of an approaching deadline. This can aid in showing the ADHDer the passing of time. Ideally, do it as a blanket reminder rather than directing it at one particular person, and do it gently — it should not be angry, condescending, frustrated, or impatient.

☐ Use a body double (see page 87).

☐ Instead of repeatedly telling an ADHDer to do something (because no one likes being told the same thing over and over), ask the person how they are getting on or if they need any help — for example, "How is it going with cleaning your room? Do you need a body double (page 87) or help getting started?"

☐ Use a visual timer.

☐ If you're making a plan with an ADHD person, or if you're an ADHD person making a plan for yourself, set the time you need to leave or complete something earlier than it needs to be. That way you'll have some wiggle room.

If you are trying to support someone with time agnosia, or with any other part of their ADHD, it is important to have a conversation first and agree on how that might best be done. Support can easily feel condescending or irritating, or can make an already frustrating and difficult situation even worse. We don't want to feel like we are "less than" others, or like we're failing at silly things for no reason, but it can feel like that sometimes, even when people are just trying to be helpful. Listen to the ADHD person and find out what will help them while still making them feel respected and understood.

Relationships

ADHDers can find relationships quite difficult to navigate. There are a number of ways in which ADHD traits can be misunderstood or misinterpreted, which may result in both parties feeling hurt, unimportant, frustrated, or unheard.

Take time agnosia, for example (see page 55). If we frequently show up late and you don't understand why, you might feel like you're less valuable or important than whatever has kept us from arriving on time. You might think we just didn't put effort or thought into making you a priority, when in reality we fully intended to be on time and did put in an effort to make that happen, but sometimes time passes a lot faster than we realize. Another example is when we might not contact you or respond to messages for an extended period of time. We may not realize how long it's been, or we may have started typing a message but been distracted, closed it, and forgotten about it due to a lack of object permanence (see page 34).

There seems to be this social rule around double-texting people — that you shouldn't send more than a couple of messages in a row without a response, even over several days. With most ADHD people, you can probably just throw that rule away. Message them! It doesn't matter if you've sent a couple of messages that they haven't yet responded to. If I never double-messaged my ADHD friends, it'd be months before I heard from them. Don't send an unnecessary amount of messages, but don't be worried about sending another message if you've already sent one and not received a response.

Masking

Masking is the act of hiding your ADHD or neurodivergent traits in order to live in a world that functions around neurotypicals. It is similar to autistic masking, but different because the traits aren't all the same.

Masking consumes a lot of attention and energy. It is a constant awareness of how you're presenting, and choosing to try to act in a way that is socially "correct." But you may or may not always be aware that you're masking.

For an ADHD person, masking might be:

☐ Thinking about when and how much eye contact you are making, because you keep getting distracted by your surroundings. It doesn't necessarily mean you aren't listening, but people often assume it does.

☐ Hiding a lack of focus by making acknowledging gestures and sounds at the appropriate intervals when you can't get your brain to actually process what is being said to you.

☐ Hiding the fact that you're getting overwhelmed by the number of things going on, both internally and externally.

☐ Hiding the frustration of desperately trying to pay attention but not being able to, for whatever reason.

☐ Forcing yourself to stay still even though that makes it harder for you to take in information.

☐ Avoiding talking so that you don't say too much or say things at the wrong time (for example, when it would interrupt another person).

☐ Withdrawing yourself to avoid being perceived as annoying or excessive.

Sometimes masking itself is what distracts and prevents us from staying focused, engaged and present. Masking is a draining process of trying to fit in, but it can be reduced through understanding and accommodations.

Some things that may be helpful:

☐ Don't rely on eye contact as an indicator of my attention. Find another way to check, or just ask.

☐ If I'm struggling to focus, find out why and then try to fix the issue — for example, by removing distractions.

☐ If I'm hyper-focused or perseverating on something, allow me to engage in that thing. Some ADHDers will still find company valuable even while they are doing something else.

☐ If, for some reason, I just cannot focus on conversation, do something that doesn't involve spoken communication.

☐ Understand that when I interrupt you, I'm not being rude or insensitive.

☐ Use words of affirmation! Remind me that you enjoy my presence and you like me for who I am. We do not have to be any particular way. We aren't too much — if I am genuinely too much for you, that's a you problem. It's not anyone's job to suppress who they are to make other people happy.

And to anyone reading this: you should never have to change who you are for another person. You are worth more than that. If who you are doesn't work for them, it's OK to let that relationship go.

Rejection Sensitive Dysphoria (RSD)

Rejection Sensitive Dysphoria (RSD) is an intense fear, worry, feeling of or sensitivity to being rejected, criticized, falling short, or messing up. RSD is quite common among individuals with ADHD. It is often very much an internal thing and not necessarily the result of anything anyone else has said or done. Although it can stem from a comment or action by another person, it can also just come from a lifetime of being labeled negatively or bullied for being different. When you get told over and over that doing a certain thing is annoying, you can start beating yourself up for it even when no one says anything about it.

RSD isn't just something that occurs in relation to other people — it can occur when we don't live up to our own standards.

RSD is painful and awful to live with. ADHDers can often be people-pleasers and perfectionists. We may avoid situations where we could make mistakes because our emotional response to being embarrassed can feel unbearable.

Individuals may find that they spend a significant amount of time after social interactions analyzing their behaviors and becoming overwhelmingly upset about the possibility of having done something wrong or being perceived negatively.

Words of affirmation and reassurance can help to ease this.

Self-esteem

A lot of ADHDers struggle with low self-esteem. Part of this is because most people really do not understand ADHD, and many go undiagnosed. As a result of this, ADHD individuals often go through life being told that they exhibit a number of flaws or undesirable characteristics. They are told that they are lazy, rude, inconsiderate, distracting, aggressive, sensitive, intense, moody, weird, annoying, too much, and too loud. Other people constantly nitpick at the person's presentation and don't take into account how much effort they are putting in just to exist.

When everyone is telling you all of these awful things about yourself, rarely pointing out any positive characteristics, it is unsurprising that you might have low self-esteem. It is also unsurprising that this would contribute to Rejection Sensitive Dysphoria (see page 64). Individuals hear these things, and they want to be liked so they try really hard to fit in. They can become overly critical of themselves when they feel as if they are failing at that.

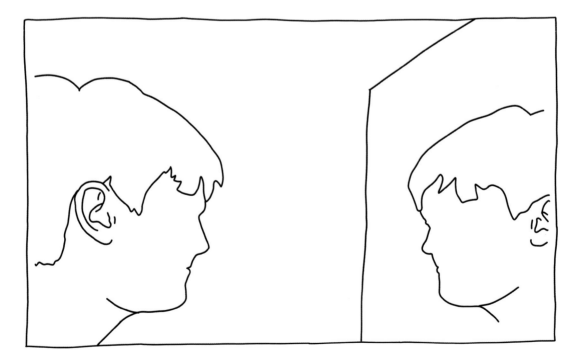

Criticism

With some of the other topics in mind — including Rejection Sensitive Dysphoria, low self-esteem and emotional dysregulation — it might be easier to understand that some ADHDers are particularly sensitive to criticism, and we may react to it in quite an intense way, either internally or externally.

I think part of the reason we are so sensitive to criticism is that we receive a lot of it, and often it's around things that other people do not understand or that aren't really fair. It also comes in the form of jokes at our expense when we do something unusual or when we make silly mistakes. We receive criticism just for being ourselves and existing, and it's painful.

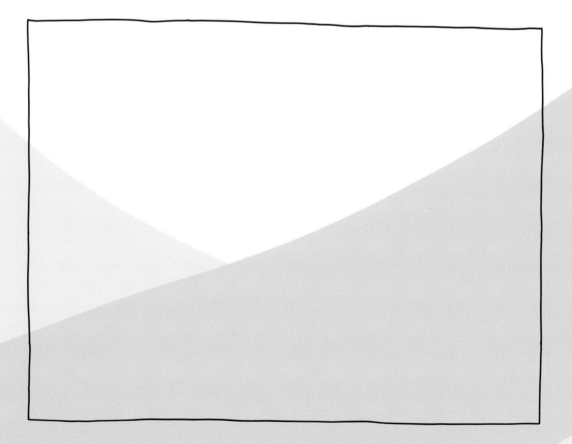

EMotional dysregulation

Emotional dysregulation is having difficulty regulating one's emotions, as well as experiencing emotions that are more extreme or intense than what would be typical or expected.

Emotional dysregulation is something that plays a part in several ADHD traits. It causes the individual to have very big feelings, both positive and negative, and those feelings can be very difficult to manage. It plays into and impacts traits and behaviors such as interrupting people, volume control, talking fast, talking excessively, concentration, perseveration, impulsivity, how we handle frustration that arises from time agnosia or forgetfulness, rejection sensitivity, self-esteem, getting to sleep, or handling things going wrong.

Life as an ADHDer can be quite intense in many ways; emotional dysregulation is just one.

Mood swings

Mood swings are sudden or unexpected changes to emotions.

Occasional, mild mood swings are a normal part of life. Things happen that can have emotional consequences that come on quickly but are short-lived. For example, let's say you're trying to sleep and a scam caller decides to repeatedly phone you. You'll probably suddenly get angry, but then when it stops you'll (usually) calm down reasonably quickly.

For some ADHD individuals, mood swings can be more common and can be paired with emotional dysregulation. So they might experience a sudden onset of intense emotions that can switch very quickly.

Reactivity and sensitivity

Between emotional dysregulation, mood swings, impulsivity, low self-esteem, and Rejection Sensitive Dysphoria, it's not uncommon for ADHDers to be perceived as overly reactive or overly sensitive. For some individuals, their feelings and overwhelm build up under the surface for an extended period of time before they come out in an outburst. Often the reaction that comes out externally is not in proportion to the thing that finally triggers it. A lot of the time there is more going on for the ADHD individual than other people realize, so they assume that the person is just being excessive and their feelings are dismissed.

On top of that, when you are impulsive, it can be particularly difficult to hold on to or control mood swings or intense emotions. It can be very easy to have a sudden reaction without thinking it through first. In these cases, the individual will often have further struggles with RSD after the event has taken place.

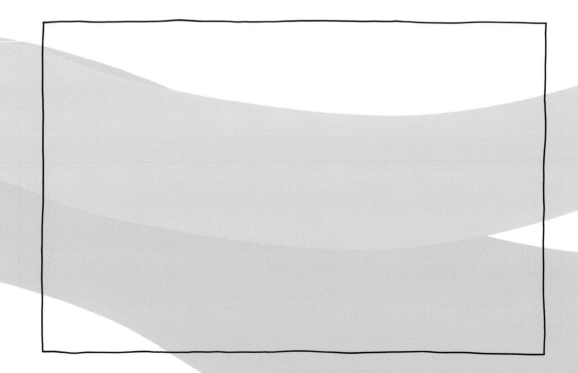

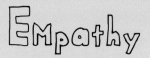

Empathy

Empathy is a topic more commonly discussed with regard to autism, but ADHDers have some shared experiences.

First, let's look at the definition of empathy. Empathy means to understand and share another person's feelings. It means to sit in that space with them and relate to how they are doing. Lacking this doesn't equal a lack of care. Some individuals, like myself, have difficulty understanding or relating to emotions or experiences that they have not been through themselves. I cannot pretend to understand, or try to put myself in someone's shoes and feel what they are feeling, because I haven't lived it myself. However, even if I may not be able to "feel" it, if I care very deeply for that person, I'll do my best to do and be what they need at the time.

Hyper-empathy: Some neurodivergent individuals are extremely empathetic. They feel things more deeply than most. However, they may not know how to express that. They may even have a hard time distinguishing between their own feelings and the feelings that they feel on behalf of another person. Sometimes what they feel can be so intense that it causes them to shut down, and this in turn can be seen as a lack of empathy.

Expressing empathy: Many neurodivergent individuals show empathy or understanding by sharing a story of a similar situation that they have experienced. They use their story to provide proof and an explanation of how they understand what the person is feeling. They use it to express the fact that the other person isn't alone in what they are experiencing. Unfortunately, neurotypicals often view this as an attempt to steal the attention, when it's not. It's to say, "I know what you're going through, and this is how I know. This is why I understand, and I'm here for you."

Unfortunately, worrying about how the way they express empathy might be perceived by another person is yet another thing that can contribute to Rejection Sensitive Dysphoria (see page 64).

Depression

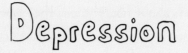

** Please note: If you are struggling with depression or think you may be heading that way, please do reach out for help. You don't have to go through it alone.

It is not uncommon for ADHD individuals to struggle with mental illnesses such as depression and anxiety. A lot of the symptoms can overlap, and when you consider some of the struggles that ADHDers experience, such as with low self-esteem and Rejection Sensitive Dysphoria, as well as low levels of dopamine, it makes sense that they might also experience depression at some point in their lives.

I'm not talking about just feeling occasional bouts of sadness — I am talking about a prolonged and debilitating condition. It involves feelings of sadness, trouble sleeping or sleeping too much, fatigue, a loss of interest in things you usually enjoy, changes to eating patterns, restlessness or slowed movements, difficulty concentrating or focusing, low self-esteem, and suicidality.

ADHD individuals often already experience fatigue, trouble with sleeping, restlessness, difficulty concentrating, or feeling bad about themselves. Without accommodations, many ADHD traits can be really draining to work around in the neurotypical structure of society. When you're slowly becoming increasingly exhausted, being misunderstood and labeled negatively, on top of having to deal with all the regular stressors and risk factors of life that everyone else has to deal with, you are somewhat more vulnerable to the possibility of becoming depressed. This is one of the reasons that putting accommodations in place is extremely important (see page 134).

Anxiety

Anxiety also has quite a bit of overlap with ADHD, and is a common comorbidity.

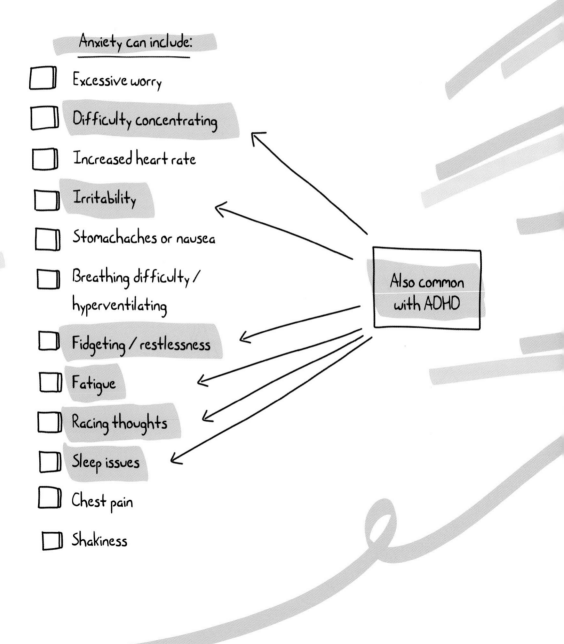

Anxiety can include:

- ☐ Excessive worry
- ☐ Difficulty concentrating
- ☐ Increased heart rate
- ☐ Irritability
- ☐ Stomachaches or nausea
- ☐ Breathing difficulty / hyperventilating
- ☐ Fidgeting / restlessness
- ☐ Fatigue
- ☐ Racing thoughts
- ☐ Sleep issues
- ☐ Chest pain
- ☐ Shakiness

Also common with ADHD

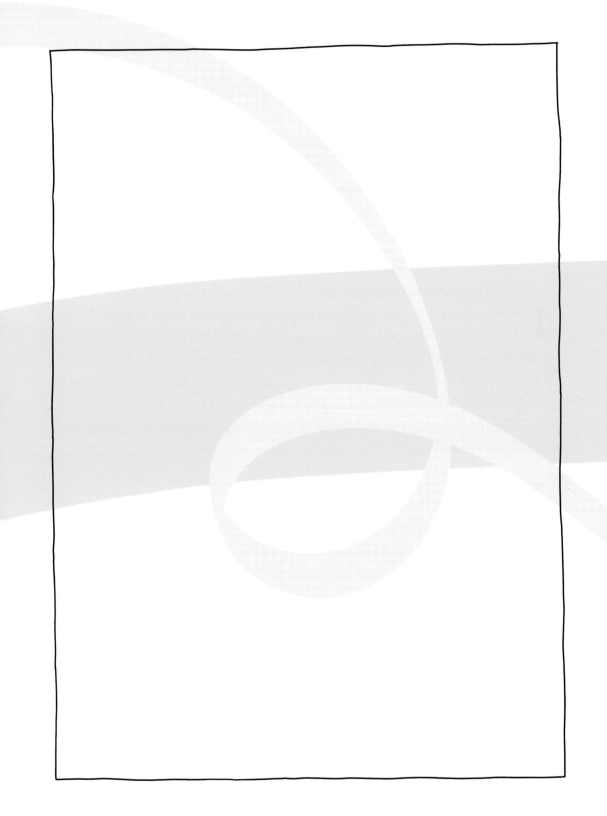

Burnout / overload

Burnout is extreme mental, physical, or emotional exhaustion, accompanied by a reduced capacity for stress of any sort. For ADHD individuals, burnout can be caused by an overload of thoughts, tasks, commitments, feelings, etc. ADHDers already have a hard time focusing and regulating their emotions, so burnout and overwhelm can make it significantly harder for them to function.

In an attempt to seek dopamine, satisfy our brains, and people-please, ADHDers will often overcommit ourselves. Many of us will be on the go all the time, taking up several new hobbies or activities, or struggling to say no to people who ask things of us. Managing our time and creating an organized plan is difficult when we struggle with executive dysfunction, and we can often find ourselves accidentally double- or triple-booked. Many of us are just not very good at slowing down and allowing time for rest — or even being comfortable with it, for that matter. On top of that, we're also often thinking about several things at once, so not only are we overcommitted physically, we're sometimes overexerting ourselves mentally — something people cannot see from the outside.

For ADHD individuals, burnout can also be caused by trying to manage, function, and fit into the neurotypical structure. ADHD brains are often extremely busy, easily distracted, and taking in a lot of information. It can be very full-on and overwhelming. Having your needs understood and accommodated, receiving support, and having the freedom to be an authentic version of yourself, without consequences, will reduce your chances of becoming overwhelmed or burned out.

However, due to the overlap between ADHD and mental illnesses such as depression and anxiety, a lot of individuals will be required to address and treat those conditions before they can access ADHD-related medication to improve their difficulties associated with having ADHD. Along with this, it can also be incredibly hard to get an ADHD diagnosis as an adult if you also have mental illness or have experienced trauma, because it is difficult to distinguish between the overlapping traits.

Sleep disturbance

ADHDers are more likely to experience issues with sleep than neurotypicals. This could be difficulty falling or staying asleep, or difficulty waking up.

Some possible reasons for this are:

ADHDers often have a hard time making or sticking to routines. Our bodies and sleep cycles rely on routines. Not having them will ultimately make it harder to get good, quality rest.

ADHDers often describe feeling more awake in the evenings than during the day. This, combined with time agnosia, can result in individuals staying up until the early hours of the morning without realizing how late it is.

ADHD often involves restlessness or racing thoughts, and that can make falling asleep very difficult.

Mental illnesses such as depression, which are common among ADHDers, can also affect sleep patterns.

Suggestions to improve sleep

☐ Even if you struggle to stick to a routine for the whole day, try to set a time (and alarm) to go to bed every night and wake up every day. If you don't succeed one day, that's OK — try again the next day.

☐ Stay off screens for an hour or two before bed. It may sound pointless, like if you're going to get off the screen you might as well go to bed. But it's not. Melatonin, the hormone associated with our sleep cycle, is affected by light. Looking at screens before bed will lower your melatonin levels, which play a very important part in getting you to sleep.

Some alternative activities:

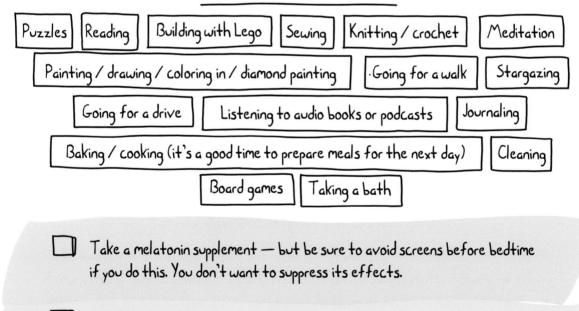

| Puzzles | Reading | Building with Lego | Sewing | Knitting / crochet | Meditation |

Painting / drawing / coloring in / diamond painting · Going for a walk · Stargazing

Going for a drive · Listening to audio books or podcasts · Journaling

Baking / cooking (it's a good time to prepare meals for the next day) · Cleaning

Board games · Taking a bath

☐ Take a melatonin supplement — but be sure to avoid screens before bedtime if you do this. You don't want to suppress its effects.

☐ Spend time outside.

☐ Avoid eating late in the evening.

☐ Exercise regularly — just not right before bed.

Executive dysfunction

Executive dysfunction is wanting to carry out a task but just not being able to. It is common for ADHD individuals to struggle with executive functioning. It impacts our ability to plan or start activities and stay on task, as well as stay organized, motivated, regulated, and able to adjust our actions according to the situation.

In a sense, what might seem like just one task for a neurotypical person might become a number of tasks that are difficult to keep in order for someone who struggles with executive functioning. For example, making a cup of coffee (one task) might become this: "I want to make coffee. That requires getting a mug out of the cupboard, coffee out of the pantry, milk from the fridge, and a spoon from the drawer. Then I have to boil the water. But the kettle is empty, so I need to fill it first. But the sink is full of dirty dishes, so I need to do the dishes. That requires taking the dishes out of the sink to fill it up with water and soap. Are there dishes anywhere else around the house? I need to clean my room…" and so on. By the end of it all, there is so much information and stuff that needs to be done that the original task feels overwhelming and paralyzing.

Even if the ADHD individual does manage to start the task, information may still be coming through faster than they can deal with it. An individual who struggles with executive dysfunction may start each new task as it comes to mind, while simultaneously forgetting about the original task. This can become dangerous if the initial task was something like cooking or ironing.

Another form of executive dysfunction is when the person is aware of their tasks but unable to prioritize them correctly. All tasks and steps are given an equal priority, which can make it hard to start anything at all. Steps may be approached out of order — for example, going to pour a drink before getting a cup out. Or the person may be unable to switch from the task that they are currently focused on to something else, even if something more urgent comes up.

Individuals may try to mask this trait, and often don't get support for it. Executive dysfunction is often very overwhelming and frustrating, and can get out of control very quickly. For example, my support worker might send me to put a plate in the dishwasher, and then come down to the kitchen a couple of minutes later only to find all of the cupboards, dishwasher and oven doors open, food on the counter, the vacuum out, and me curled on the floor, watching videos on my phone and almost in tears because I'm overwhelmed at how many tasks my brain is trying to do at once.

However, it is something that can be somewhat managed and helped through therapy, medication, and body doubling (see page 87) as well as appropriate tools, support, and adjustments.

Some ways to help with
executive dysfunction:

Make a plan for your day or
week. (It may be easier to get
someone to help you with this
— and hold you accountable
for sticking to it.) ☐

Have step-by-step, visual
instructions for tasks that
you need to do regularly. ☐

Make a checklist of things
that you need to get done. ☐

Ask for support to appropriately
prioritize and lay out tasks. This is
something that parents, teachers,
and employers can do to accommodate
ADHD individuals. Write things out
in order of importance, so that the
tasks are already organized. This
will ease one of the challenges with
starting and staying on task. ☐

Download an app that
gives you reminders
☐ about tasks.

Before starting a task or project,
write each "step" on a sticky note.
From there you can move them into a
logical order. Then you can get started,
and after you complete each step, you
can remove the corresponding note.

☐

Trouble with Making or sticking to routines

Making a routine requires focus, executive functioning, and motivation. Sticking to a routine requires an awareness of time and remembering the plan. It also relies on the individual not getting distracted or hyper-fixating on something. There is sometimes no way to plan a routine in such a way that ensures that you will be getting enough dopamine to actually have the motivation to follow through with it. You never really know what might be enjoyable or what you might end up focused on, on any given day. Also, the ADHD brain gets bored very easily, so a routine that is the same every week can quickly become unmanageable.

This is one trait that creates a bit of a clash when you are also autistic. Autistics have a need for structure, routine, and familiarity, and ADHDers struggle to follow routine or sameness. When you have both at the same time, it becomes a bit of a battle to ensure that all needs are being met.

Disorganization

ADHDers are often disorganized.

Sometimes, though, we might just be chaotically organized.

With ADHD, disorganization stems from a number of traits, such as forgetfulness, lack of object permanence, distractibility, time agnosia, and executive dysfunction.

When it comes to managing this, it may not look the same as it would for a neurotypical. We function differently, therefore the tools that help neurotypical people won't necessarily help an ADHDer.

So, for us, being organized may mean: having a "messy" desk or room, so that we know where everything is; doing multiple tasks at the same time; switching between tasks to keep focus and motivation; or doing things at the very last minute, when the adrenaline of a fast-approaching deadline helps us to stay focused and get the job done.

We may look disorganized, but that isn't always the case. We need to do what works for our brains, and that doesn't always work for everyone else.

Your version of organized isn't necessarily the same as mine!

Body doubling enilduob ydoB

Body doubling is a simple concept. It is having another person present while we are doing a chore or task. The person doesn't necessarily have to be helping — all they have to do is be there and be aware that we're struggling to start or complete a task.

Having someone else present and aware of the situation helps to increase our accountability. The person acts as a reminder of the task that we're meant to be doing. Having a conversation can also help to make boring tasks more enjoyable, and in a situation where everything just becomes overwhelming and we don't know where to start, or we're having a hard time staying on task, the body double can act as a sounding board to help get things in order or make suggestions about what our next step should be.

ADHD paralysis

ADHD paralysis is a concept closely tied to executive dysfunction. It is a type of shutdown where you simply cannot get yourself to do something or make a decision. Some describe it as feeling like being tied or weighed down.

It is often the result of an overwhelming number of thoughts, or the frustration that comes with executive dysfunction, where you want or need to get things done but just can't. An example might be that I am fully aware that I have food on the stove that is burning, but my brain is so busy with thoughts of all of the steps involved in everything else my brain is telling me I need to do that I physically cannot do anything. My brain is telling me to do all of these things that I literally cannot do all at once, but they all kind of end up being given equal priority, and that makes it difficult to actually start any of them. Logically, I know that dealing with the burning food is the priority, but I'm so overwhelmed by everything else that I need to do that it's difficult switching my attention to the one thing that needs to be taken care of immediately.

There are also times when the paralysis is not caused by overwhelm but rather a lack of dopamine (see page 96). A lack of dopamine results in a lack of motivation, even if you want or need to get things done — especially when it comes to boring tasks.

ADHD paralysis is often invisible to everyone else. You might see an ADHD individual sitting on the couch staring at their phone when they need to get things done and just think they are being lazy, when in reality they often actually want to get up and be productive, they just can't.

Laziness

ADHDers are often labeled as lazy. We are told that we forget things because we're too lazy to pay attention, to listen, to double-check to ensure we have all our belongings. We are called lazy for having messy rooms, desks, or lockers. We are called lazy for not completing chores or work, when in fact we are fighting our own brains and feelings of overwhelm to try to plan and start those tasks. We are called lazy for not showing initiative, or for deciding that we don't have the capacity to do favors for other people.

In fact, we can be putting in a significant amount of mental energy because we desperately want to get things done, but then someone who cannot see that internal battle tells us that we are just not making enough effort. This is exhausting, invalidating, and upsetting. It makes it even harder to get things done, because while we're trying to get our minds in order and muster up an ounce of motivation, we're also beating ourselves up for not being good enough.

By definition, being lazy means that you are unwilling to work or put in effort. ADHDers are not lazy. We would often very much like to be productive and complete the boring tasks that we are not interested in but we know are a part of life.

People often look only at the "easy" things that we're not managing to do, and not at the bigger things that we're doing with ease. I very much would like to get my dishes done or tidy my room or cook a proper meal on my own, but that's hard when you have low levels of dopamine. This is one reason why choosing a career doing something you enjoy or are interested in can be particularly important for ADHD individuals.

Waiting Mode

A common experience among ADHD individuals is being in a kind of waiting mode — being stuck unable to do anything else when you have another commitment at a set time. Having a twenty-minute doctor's appointment scheduled for 3p.m. can consume an entire day.

Here are some possible reasons for this:

☐ I do not want to accidentally miss or forget about my commitment.

☐ Doing another task is too stressful because I might lose track of time.

☐ I am very aware of the time, so everything feels slow and boring.

☐ I am anxious about it, and the anxiety is distracting me.

☐ I can't think about or focus on anything else.

☐ I am thinking through and perseverating on all of the steps involved in attending or participating in the commitment, for example, how I'm getting there, what I need to remember to bring with me, or what I need to say when I'm there.

☐ I am unsure what time my commitment is happening, so I can't start another task because I may not have enough time to complete it.

☐ The thought of being interrupted or having to switch tasks when I've had to put effort into focusing is stressful and exhausting.

Being told what to do

Many ADHD individuals will absolutely hate being told what to do. To be fair, no one likes being instructed to do things, but ADHDers are sometimes particularly sensitive to it.

It makes sense, though. Often we're already very aware that we're not doing all of the things we need to do. Often we're already fighting our brains to get something done, and being told to do it only makes us feel inferior or further frustrated, because we are trying.

On top of that, our motivation often comes from interest, while neurotypical motivation often comes from importance. Sometimes, if you tell me to do something, you are taking away any chance of that task being interest-based. You are turning it into a "have to do" task, which is more related to importance.

We may also hate being told what to do because when people give us instructions they don't understand that our brains function differently from theirs. They are often trying to get us to do things that work for them but not for us.

The other thing about this is that when a neurotypical person refuses to do something (as an adult), it is often seen as a positive trait — a sign of having confidence and strong boundaries. But when an ADHDer refuses to do something, it's put down to their ADHD being a negative trait and they are seen as being rude or difficult.

One way around this is to rephrase instructions into questions. Instead of "Do your homework," maybe say, "Do you need any help with your homework?" or "How are you getting on with your homework?" Instead of "Vacuum the house" or "You need to take out the trash," say "Hey, I'm going to do some cleaning — can you please help out and keep me company?" We know the value of getting things done alongside other people, and we like being wanted and needed.

Dopamine

Dopamine is a monoamine neurotransmitter.

Neurotransmitters are chemical messengers in the brain that are vital to our ability to function.

Monoamine neurotransmitters include serotonin, histamine, norepinephrine, and dopamine. Each of these has an important role to play, but dopamine plays a part in motivation, pleasure, mood, memory, movement, and attention, among other things.

Dopamine is what makes us feel good and gives us motivation when we do something pleasurable. When we do something we enjoy, we get a dopamine rush.

ADHDers may have low levels of dopamine, and that can mean we often struggle with motivation, focus, and energy. This is why we are interest-driven (see page 98). Doing something that we are interested in and that we enjoy triggers a release of dopamine, which helps us to function and stay motivated.

Ways to get dopamine

** Please note: Not all of the things listed below are healthy. I am simply listing them because it might explain certain behaviors of those who are dopamine-seeking. These are just some examples; there are lots of things that can trigger a dopamine release.

- [ ] Shopping
- [ ] Sex
- [ ] Listening to music
- [ ] Some medications
- [ ] Doing something new
- [ ] Completing a task — even a small one
- [ ] Exercising
- [ ] Achieving something
- [ ] Eating sugary foods
- [ ] Gambling
- [ ] Doing almost anything that you enjoy
- [ ] Nicotine
- [ ] Receiving positive feedback
- [ ] Playing video games

Interest-based vs. importance-based nervous system

This is a topic that I find really interesting, but I encourage you to do your own research on this to gain a full understanding of it, because I am not a professional in any way.

Many neurodivergents have an interest-based nervous system, while neurotypicals tend to have an importance-based nervous system. What this means is that, for a neurodivergent, motivation to complete a task is triggered by their interest. That interest can be created by curiosity, being challenged, a topic they find fascinating, something that falls within their core values, etc. When the interest wears off, so does the motivation. This makes it really difficult for them to do anything that they do not find interesting.

Neurotypicals, however, frequently gain their motivation to complete a task based on its importance: things that are important to them, to their boss, for their goals, for personal gain, or, again, something that falls within their core values. So their way of prioritizing tasks might be determined by what is most important to them at the time.

This can sometimes lead to a lack of understanding between people who are motivated in different ways.

To manage this, you can use to-do lists, sticker charts, and reward systems. Crossing things off or having a visual representation of the completion of a task will help to trigger a dopamine release, and thus help to keep you motivated and focused. You are never too old to use tools like this that work for your brain and help you to do life.

Boredom

No one likes feeling bored. Everyone finds boredom to be uncomfortable, but most people can manage it. For example, a neurotypical sitting through a boring lecture will probably cope reasonably fine and be able to stick it out until the end. They might be bored, but they can still usually take in the information. For ADHD individuals, boredom can be painful, stressful, frustrating, anxiety-provoking, and intolerable — especially if the boring thing is important. It can be incredibly overwhelming and infuriating when you cannot get yourself to focus on something that you *need* to focus on.

Boring tasks do not trigger a dopamine release. They, therefore, do not trigger motivation. For ADHD individuals with low levels of dopamine, doing a boring task means having no motivation to continue with that task, but doing something stimulating means feeling rewarded. It's a choice between doing the thing that I have absolutely no immediate incentive for, and which feels really yuck, or doing the thing that literally rewards my brain with a feel-good hormone.

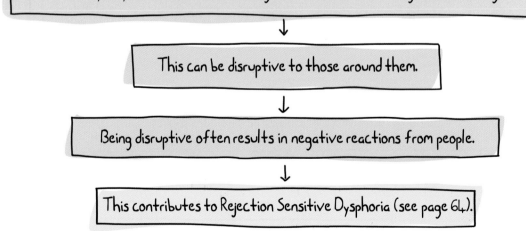

Combined with impulsivity, this can mean that when the ADHD individual gets bored they may act out or do something that is more interesting or stimulating.

↓

This can be disruptive to those around them.

↓

Being disruptive often results in negative reactions from people.

↓

This contributes to Rejection Sensitive Dysphoria (see page 64).

People often don't understand that we're not intentionally being annoying. It's also not an easy decision to choose to not seek stimulation. It's not as simple as just choosing not to "misbehave." We're essentially being told to suffer in silence, sit still, and be quiet instead of being given tools to cope or stay engaged, because people do not understand how it feels.

Boredom feels:

- ☐ Frustrating
- ☐ Uncomfortable
- ☐ Painful
- ☐ Stressful
- ☐ Anxiety-provoking
- ☐ Overwhelming
- ☐ Tiring
- ☐ Fine
- ☐ Impossible to manage or sit with
- ☐
- ☐

Things that may help when doing something boring:

- ☐ Being able to move around
- ☐ Active seating (Swiss ball, wobble stool, spinning chair)
- ☐ Body doubling
- ☐ Listening to music
- ☐ Having a conversation or company at the same time
- ☐ Turning it into a game (What is the longest piece of potato peel I can create? How many times does the lecturer say a certain word?)
- ☐ Turn it into a sticker chart or to-do list — even with small tasks like "get the washing out of the machine" or "write two hundred words of my assignment." It feels rewarding to check things off.
- ☐

Reward systems

Reward systems are tricky, because they should not act as punishment if you *don't* do something (for example, "If I don't take the trash out, then I don't get to eat my favorite food"). The purpose of a reward system is to create an incentive to do things that do not trigger a dopamine release and are therefore difficult for the ADHDer to complete. It should not add more stress and frustration to an already frustrating situation.

Nor should reward systems act to train you out of being who you are (for example, "If you sit still and be quiet then you get ...") or be a replacement for accommodations. Also, caution should be taken around using food as a reward, as that can contribute to unhealthy eating habits and beliefs.

Obviously, it's easier to use reward systems for children, as they do not have the means to simply reward themselves with their own money. So having reward systems for yourself as an adult may look a bit different.

In my case, I might decide that once I've done five of my chores around the house then I can spend time building Lego. That's not to say that if I *don't* do the chores, I can't build Lego, but it means that if I *do* do the chores, I know I'll enjoy the Lego more because my brain won't be fixated on the fact that I haven't completed certain tasks that need to get done. It's telling my brain that I'm allowed to stop thinking about all the things I "should" be doing because I'm "rewarding" myself for achieving something. Having a reward in place doesn't mean I have to do the chores on my own (without a body double, for example). I'm still allowed accommodations.

Another example might be deciding that once I have attended a meeting or class that is boring, I'll go get a bubble tea or go to the trampoline park. It's a way to tell my brain that yes, this thing is boring, but it's OK because I'll make up for it afterward. It's less of a "reward" for doing what I need to do and more of a way to ensure that my needs are being met; it's not based on my performance or how well or badly I do while I am at that meeting or class.

However, reward systems (or even punishments, for that matter) are counter-productive and useless if the underlying difficulties have not been identified and addressed. A reward is not going to help me magically figure out the order of all of the steps of things that are overwhelming my brain. A reward is not going to magically remove impulsivity or hyperactivity. Rewards are simply a tool that can aid in adding motivation where there isn't any.

Trouble finishing projects or tasks

Many ADHDers have trouble finishing projects. Often, our interest (and therefore motivation) wears off before we can complete things, or sometimes there was never any interest and we've run out of capacity or energy to get ourselves to do something that we're not motivated to do. Also, finishing projects often requires extra focus because it's the part where there's more detail or smaller things to think about.

Other times, we may start a task because it will fill a need. But once the need is filled, the task is no longer desirable. For example, I may start cleaning the entire house because it is a way to release restlessness and hyperactivity and my brain is seeking stimulation through moving around and being on the go. But as soon as my brain has the stimulation it needs, I'll no longer have the energy to finish what probably ended up being several tasks that I got only halfway through (or made worse).

Also, when something is interesting to us, it's not always going to remain interesting every single time we do it or look at it. I can write a story because that's enjoyable, but then tidying it up and turning it into a finished product ... that's boring, because I already know what's in the story. I can start painting a picture and it's fun, but after staring at the same thing for a while or getting an idea of what it would look like when it's finished, it just becomes uninteresting.

This is actually why some ADHD individuals will be more efficient at certain tasks, such as assignments or writing — we do not have the interest to go over things multiple times so we skip the "draft" step and dive into it the first time around. However, being efficient doesn't necessarily mean getting things done before others. Many ADHDers work best under time pressure, and will leave their work until the very last minute because a fast-approaching deadline is when they are motivated to get their work done.

Spontaneity

Spontaneity goes hand in hand with impulsivity. In fact, they are synonyms. Both mean acting with little to no planning. I think the main difference in the way we use the terms would be that impulsivity refers to an urge that's hard to resist, whereas spontaneity can be more controlled and is sometimes less likely to be regrettable.

Being spontaneous is not uncommon for ADHD individuals. When you aren't sticking to a routine or making a plan for the day, it's easier to just go with the flow of things and do whatever comes up. It keeps things interesting and fun and is an easy source of dopamine.

However, this is not the most fun trait if you are also autistic. My ADHD would absolutely love going on a spontaneous road trip on a Saturday morning when my friends all realize they have the day free. My autism, however, stresses out at the idea of not having prepared for that or made a detailed plan for where exactly we are going and what time I will get back.

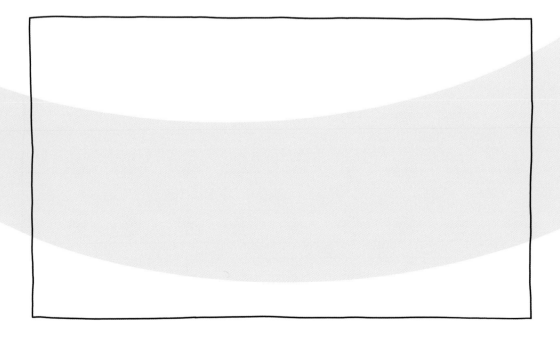

Sugar

Many ADHD individuals will have a bit of a sweet tooth. Sugar is something that triggers a release of dopamine, so eating foods that are high in sugar feels very rewarding. Unfortunately, when we regularly consume sugar, our brains develop a tolerance to it and require more of it to achieve the same "high." This can obviously be very unhealthy and can turn into excessive cravings or addiction.

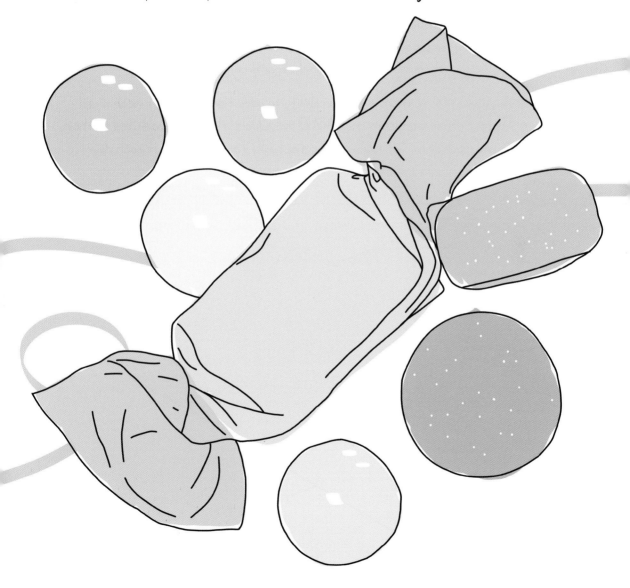

Addiction

ADHD individuals can be particularly vulnerable to addiction. It makes sense when you consider their potentially low levels of dopamine, intolerance for boredom, impulsivity, anxiety, and the fact that self-esteem issues or Rejection Sensitive Dysphoria (see page 64) can contribute to feelings of isolation or not belonging.

Things that are addictive are often things that give a dopamine hit. They relieve or release intense feelings such as anxiety, even if only briefly. Some addictions can also be calming or can slow things down, and some addictive behaviors carry a social element to them (such as social drinking or drug-taking).

However, just because there's a vulnerability to addiction, it doesn't mean it will happen. There is often a concern that ADHD individuals will become addicted to their prescribed medication, yet many of them actually forget to take it each day.

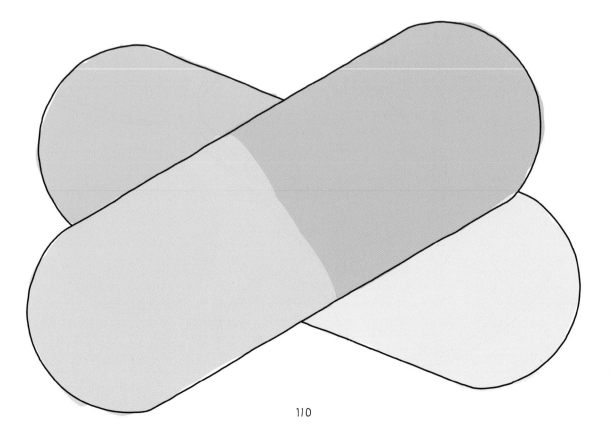

Stimulation

The ADHD brain often craves stimulation. It craves dopamine, movement, busyness, or a place to direct mental energy that can otherwise become overwhelming. Some of us will constantly need something, often multiple sources of stimulation at any given time. Some people will find that they cannot simply sit and watch a movie or TV show — they need to be doing something else at the same time. For example, I might watch TV, play a game on my phone, and knit at the same time.

Sensory overload

Unfortunately, with everything going on in our minds — how much information we take in and our constant search for stimulation, often through multiple sources — we can become overstimulated or experience sensory overload. This feeling of overwhelm may be difficult to notice until it becomes too much. It can happen very quickly, or build up over an extended period of time. It can also be difficult to differentiate between sensory processing issues and ADHD, as they may result in similar behaviors, such as difficulty with focusing, feeling like there's too much going on, getting extremely emotional, having outbursts, or seeking sensory stimulation.

However, as someone with both ADHD and Sensory Processing Disorder, I can say that ADHD absolutely exacerbates my sensory difficulties — it's like an excitable and energetic golden retriever who's developed the ability to talk and will not leave me alone.

Some days I desperately wish I could tell my brain to just shut up. I don't want to listen to the same line of a song over and over again, think about some random conversation I had four years ago, the chores I'm meant to be doing, some stupid mistake I made yesterday, when I last made eye contact with someone, what that weird sound was that I heard last Tuesday, what my pet might be up to in this moment, and all of the things I need to get done today — all while I'm standing in the supermarket trying to decide which flavor of chips I want to buy.

So while we may crave stimulation, it can also be incredibly exhausting.

Clumsiness

Many ADHD individuals are quite clumsy. They frequently bump or walk into things and get unexplained bruises and injuries. This may be because they are too distracted to pay attention to their surroundings, or they may just move around quite quickly and walk into table corners or door frames.

To be fair, when individuals are by nature impulsive and restless, they are probably more vulnerable or prone to getting hurt. And when you're forgetful or distractible you might not remember where bruises came from. But being clumsy, bumping into things or not being aware that you are getting (or have been) injured can also be related to your proprioceptive, vestibular, and interoceptive systems.

Proprioception

Proprioception is the awareness of our body in relation to space and objects, as well as the awareness of how our body is positioned and how much force we are using. Issues with proprioception can result in clumsiness, bumping into things, being too rough, using too much force, difficulty with motor skills, etc.

Issues with proprioception can present in many different ways. For me, as an autistic person with ADHD and Sensory Processing Disorder, it means that I cannot feel how my body is positioned unless I am touching a stable surface. I know how to tell my body to move into different positions, but I cannot feel the difference between them. For example, if I am in a handstand, having my legs straight and together feels the same as having them bent and apart. I also struggle to tell how tight my grip is, and I often walk into things.

Proprioceptive input is anything that provides intense sensation or input to the muscles and joints. Activities that provide proprioceptive input include using a weighted blanket, having a tight hug, walking on tiptoes, chewing, interacting with things that provide pressure (like squeezing into small spaces), etc. Proprioceptive input is calming for many people.

Vestibular system

The vestibular system uses receptors in the inner ear to send information to the brain about head position, balance, movement in space, and changes to the speed at which we are moving. Issues with the vestibular system can result in an avoidance of intense vestibular activities such as spinning or jumping, or it can result in things like poor balance, seeming to never get dizzy when spinning, constantly moving, seeking out more powerful forms of vestibular input, etc. The way in which this presents itself depends on whether the individual is under- or overprocessing information from the receptors in their inner ear. Vestibular input is anything that engages those receptors — swinging, spinning, climbing, jumping, being upside down, balancing, etc.

Difficulty with the vestibular system is only one possible explanation for clumsiness or frequent engagement in movement-seeking. Intense vestibular input can also be used as a form of self-regulation for some individuals. Others will find that it has quite the opposite effect.

Interoception

Interoception is the awareness of what is going on inside our body. It tells us when we are hungry, full, nauseated, too hot, too cold, need to go to the toilet, need to sleep, etc. Having difficulty with interoception can mean that you don't feel those things, can't identify what different sensations are, or don't interpret them correctly. This can mean that individuals may forget to do certain vital tasks like eating or going to the toilet, or may not be aware of the steps that need to be taken in order to keep their body well.

Difficulties with interoception can also affect our perception of pain, as well as our breathing rate and heart rate.

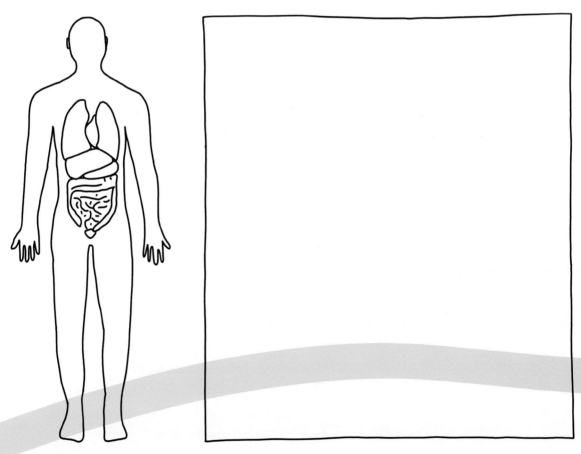

Listening

Listening is something that can be just as frustrating for us as it is for the person who is trying to talk to us. We know that there are social rules and behaviors that people look for to feel heard, such as eye contact or not doing other tasks at the same time. But these behaviors aren't necessarily indicators of attention, and can be difficult for many neurodivergent people, for different reasons. Trying to listen while following all the other social requirements that come with that can be very challenging or even impossible — but when we listen in a way that works for us, people can think we're being rude, and can become frustrated trying to get our attention when they already have it.

ADHDers are often easily distracted, so we may not be looking directly at you when you are talking. It doesn't necessarily mean we aren't listening.

We are often very restless and fidgety. Moving, doing another task or looking around doesn't mean we're uninterested in what you're saying. Sometimes getting up and doing another activity while you are talking is our way of making an effort to actually listen to you. It's not necessarily that what you're saying is boring, but just sitting and listening is often not enough stimulation to satisfy our brains.

Our thoughts run very quickly. You might have said something, and I've thought about it and gone off on several different tangents in my mind stemming from what you've said. Then the thing that I actually say out loud in response might seem entirely unrelated. Sometimes it is unrelated, because there is a lot going on in my mind, but it doesn't always mean that I have not processed what you've said.

Sometimes the reason I might say something unrelated is because my mind is stuck on a thought and I can't listen until I get it out, or I might have wanted to say something earlier in the conversation but not found a gap to say it, and now the conversation has moved on and I don't know what else to do.

To be fair, sometimes we just aren't listening or processing what is being said. Sometimes we are desperately trying to listen but nothing is sticking. It can be hard to tell when we're genuinely paying attention and when we're not. And when we're not, it's usually not because we're purposely ignoring you. Often, it's not something that is easy to control and we do feel awful when that hurts someone.

You can help me by:

☐ Allowing me to move around or do another activity while you talk to me.

☐ Asking if now is a good time to have a conversation — if not, maybe write things down for me to look at later. There's not much point in trying to have a conversation when I won't be able to give you my full attention.

☐ Texting me instead of phoning — or checking before you call.

☐ Kindly asking me if you're worried I'm not paying attention. It depends on what our relationship is like, but you could say, for example, "Just checking that you've got all of that? Do I need to go back and repeat anything?"

☐ Removing or walking away from things that are distracting me.

☐ Kindly telling me if there's something I can do to make you feel more heard, and giving me a chance to do that. For example, say "I'm really upset right now and I just need you to sit with me and chat." If we know that we're needed or wanted in some way, it's easier for us to stay focused. But also, respect boundaries. If a person does not have the capacity to have a conversation or support someone else, that is not rude. It is important that they look after themselves and don't constantly take on more than they can handle.

Learning styles

Everyone learns and processes information in different ways. It is unrealistic to expect every individual to be able to achieve the same result when given the same tools. Just because it's easy for you to learn from reading a page of information, it doesn't mean that's easy for someone else. Or just because it's easy for you to learn from a lecture, it doesn't mean that someone else wasn't paying enough attention if they don't also learn that way.

There are four learning styles: reading / writing; kinesthetic (learning by doing or moving); auditory (hearing spoken information); and visual (pictures and diagrams). Most people will use a combination of their senses to learn, but will usually favor one.

Kinesthetic learning is fairly common among ADHD individuals, but using a combination of learning styles can help to ensure that the information is going to be absorbed one way or another.

Some suggestions that may be helpful:

- [ ] Use pictures and diagrams and colors.

- [ ] Create variation in the layout of large amounts of text.

- [ ] When you give information verbally, also give it in a written and visual form.

- [ ] Use audio books.

- [ ] Have conversations about learning or put information into a song.

- [ ] Turn information into movements. My biology teacher did this for the definition of osmosis and I've never forgotten it.

- [ ] If possible, when teaching a new task or activity, provide written steps with diagrams, give a demonstration while talking through what you're doing, and then let the learner do it themselves or physically interact with what's going on. This covers all four learning styles.

Reading

Reading can be very difficult for ADHD individuals. We can easily lose track of where we're up to on the page, skip lines or words, forget parts of the story, be too distracted to take in information and have to read it over and over again, or simply find it too boring to sit and stare at pages that usually all look pretty much the same. When your mind struggles to focus on one thing, it can also be difficult to visualize only the stories in your mind and nothing else. It can be very frustrating, trying to maintain focus on reading, and it's easy to zone out.

If you are someone who feels like you are failing or useless because you struggle with reading, don't be too hard on yourself. I basically failed almost every reading comprehension test I did as a child, and I read only one book in the four years of high school that I did — and yet, here I am, writing a book for you. Keep trying. Don't give up. Don't compare yourself to everyone else.

Strategies that might help:

☐ Use your finger or a bookmark to keep track of where you are up to.

☐ Listen to audio books. I find that listening to an audio book while following along with the physical book in front of me gives me the greatest chance of taking in the information.

☐ Take key notes along the way.

☐ Draw small pictures or doodles in the book that match what that page is talking about. If you can't draw directly on the book, use sticky notes. This will give visual reminders of information but also create some variation in the appearance of each page.

☐ Read while standing or walking.

☐ Read out loud (although some ADHD individuals find that when they read out loud, they aren't actually processing anything they're saying).

☐ Have noise going in the background, as long as you don't find it distracting.

☐ Break the reading task into small achievements, for example, "read ten pages." This also gives you more stopping and starting points than just the ends of chapters.

☐ If reading a large novel just isn't doable, don't beat yourself up. Maybe try graphic novels or books that have a unique layout.

☐

☐

Medication

Most medications prescribed to manage certain traits associated with ADHD are stimulants. These include methylphenidate (Ritalin, Concerta, Methylin, Rubifen), dextroamphetamine, dexmethylphenidate (Focalin) and amphetamine. Adderall is a combination of dextroamphetamine and amphetamine.

These medications all have slight differences, but essentially they work by increasing the concentration of dopamine and norepinephrine. This helps to reduce hyperactivity, impulsivity and difficulty concentrating in individuals with ADHD, but the medications don't work for everyone. They can also aggravate some traits, such as anxiety.

When taking medication, a lot of ADHD individuals describe a quietness in their mind that they didn't know was possible (similar to the typical experience for neurotypicals). It is important to remember that the way a neurotypical might experience the effects of these medications is not the same as how an ADHD individual might experience them.

The purpose of medication is not to eliminate or cure ADHD, but to help with some of the difficulties. It is not a magic fix for all differences, issues, and learned behaviors or habits.

ADHD medications are often hard to access or cost too much. It can be difficult to get an ADHD diagnosis in adulthood, and if you're also struggling with mental health issues, then ADHD medications may not be the most suitable option.

Medication side effects

Obviously each type of medication will have its own set of possible side effects. As with many medications there are a lot of things that could happen, but here are some to consider:

☐ Loss of appetite. It's already pretty easy to get distracted and forget to eat when you aren't taking medication, so if your medication causes loss of appetite it can be even harder to remember to eat. It is essential to ensure that you are still eating properly and putting tools in place to remind you to eat throughout the day.

☐ Weight loss   ☐ Nausea   ☐ Headaches   ☐ Dizziness

☐ Insomnia   ☐ Anxiety   ☐ Constipation   ☐ Irritability

Some individuals will also struggle with coming down from medication (i.e., when it starts wearing off for the day). They may be more emotional, irritable, or tired, and it can be quite intense. Consuming high-protein foods can help with this.

Each individual will have different experiences. Sometimes the pros outweigh the cons, and sometimes they don't. The first medication you try may not be ideal for you, and it may take a bit of time to figure out what works best.

My experience with Medication

For me, as an AuDHD adult, when I'm not taking medication it's as if every thought, song, memory, or emotion is a person or being inside my head. They're crowding the space in my brain and they never shut up. When I take methylphenidate, it's as if someone has come into my brain, gathered everyone together and shoved them all into a cupboard. That process is somewhat uncomfortable because it feels like an intense amount of energy is being trapped in a very confined space. But once the cupboard door is closed, I have room to breathe and actually choose what I want to think about. Nothing comes into that space unless I go looking for it. It's not silent — the thoughts haven't shut up — but they're confined and muffled and I can ignore them.

When the medication starts wearing off, it's as if the cupboard door is opening and everyone is slowly crowding back into the room. That part is tiring and kind of depressing because, ready or not, you're replacing that quietness, focus, and motivation with excessive, useless, and painful noise. I have found this particular aspect more manageable when taking the sustained-release form of the medication.

In my experience, ADHD medication reduces my overstimulation by turning down the noise in my brain, giving me a greater capacity to manage external stimulation. It also has a significant impact on my emotional regulation and executive functioning. But it does come with some adverse effects. I find that once the medication wears off, I'm often stuck in either hyper-focus or ADHD paralysis, neither of which I have much control over. On top of that, neutralising some of my ADHD tendencies means that some of my autistic traits are intensified. For example, while on medication, transitions are significantly harder for me to deal with. I need more time to prepare to switch between environments or tasks.

For me, the benefits of ADHD medication outweigh the negatives and it has made a big difference to my quality of life.

Caffeine

Caffeine is a stimulant, and for some ADHDers it can have a similar effect to ADHD medication. Caffeine is obviously not going to be as strong or necessarily as effective as ADHD medication, but it can be helpful for some people who may not have access to or want medication.

Caffeine can help some ADHDers to focus and be calmer, and some even find that caffeine makes them sleepy — but that does not mean it's a good idea to drink it late in the day or at night.

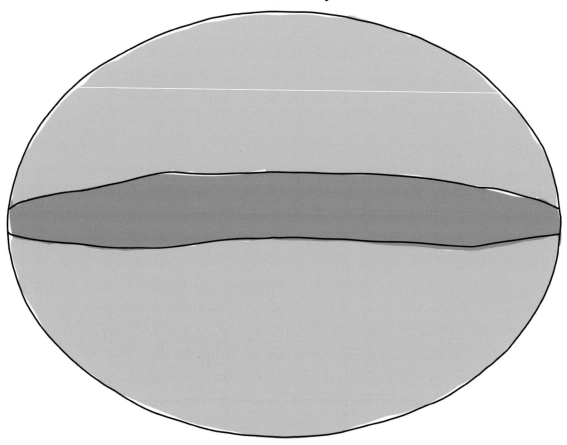

Presentation and age

All too often when it comes to neurodivergence, people seem to hold this false belief that individuals will present the same way regardless of their age. We hear things like, "You can't have ADHD because my five-year-old son has ADHD and you're nothing like him" or "You're faking, because you're not nearly as hyperactive as my child." We even get told that we couldn't possibly be neurodivergent because our traits don't match someone our own age.

An adult (or even an older child) is not going to act the same as a young child. As we go through life, just like everyone else, we learn how to cope with certain things, we learn what behavior is appropriate and what is not, and many of us learn to mask.

As an AFAB [assigned female at birth] adult, I am not going to present or behave in the same way as a school-aged boy. I've learned self-awareness, maturity, and societal norms. I've collected tools over many years to manage and function through life.

Regardless, every neurodivergent person will have different experiences, just as every neurotypical person will. Are you exactly the same as every single one of your coworkers? Almost definitely not. We all have different personalities and traits. We are all still humans.

Myths

"Only children have ADHD" —
Neurodivergent children turn
into neurodivergent adults, but
behaviors change and people
find tools to manage
daily life.

"Everyone is a little ADHD" —
ADHD is a neurodevelopmental condition.
You either have it or you don't. However, traits
associated with ADHD are still human traits. Just
because it's an ADHD behavior, it does not mean
that no one else experiences it. The difference
comes with the combination, severity, and
frequency of certain traits and behaviors.

"ADHD is caused by
bad parenting"

"It's not ADHD, they are just lazy"

"ADHD is a male diagnosis" —
Females often go undiagnosed or misdiagnosed
because ADHD looks different in females
than it does in males.

"ADHDers just need more
discipline"

"You have to
be hyperactive to have ADHD" —
ADHD has multiple presentations;
hyperactivity is just one.

"ADHDers just need to try
harder"

"You can't have ADHD if you do well at school" —
Just because it's significantly harder to focus or to manage
executive functioning (among other things), this does not
automatically mean we are incapable of achieving things.

"ADHD is just an excuse for
bad behavior"

Importance of accommodations / adjustments

A failure to meet an individual's needs will always have negative consequences. Expecting an individual whose needs are not being accommodated to live up to the same standards as someone whose needs are being met will only result in the downfall of their well-being. For example, you can't expect a starving child to behave the same as a child who is well fed, or a d/Deaf person to be able to learn from a spoken lecture without a translator or hearing aids.

I will always maintain that neurodivergence or disabilities are not excuses, they are explanations. When you have an explanation, you have the ability to do something about it. Putting the appropriate accommodations and adjustments in place for individuals with disabilities will reduce the likelihood of overwhelm or burnout and, in turn, problematic or disruptive behaviors.

It is important to remember that none of these traits are isolated. When an individual lashes out as a result of impulsivity, it isn't just this that they are dealing with. They could be dealing with any number of the other traits associated with ADHD, as well as the vast number of stressors that any person could come across, which can reduce their capacity to handle things. So if you accommodate them and make things easier in other areas, there's more room for them to work on managing things that you can't make accommodations for.

Often accommodations benefit everyone, not just disabled people. This is good, but we also need to ensure that when accommodations are put in place they are not designed in a way that still leaves the disabled person at a disadvantage in comparison to everyone else.

For example, if a disabled person needs more time to complete exams than others do, giving extra time to everyone rather than just the individual will still leave the disabled person at a disadvantage. But if you provide subtitles and transcripts, if you ensure that the built environment (e.g., doorways, footpaths, and rooms) is accessible to a range of levels of mobility, and if you allow active seating or allow individuals to communicate, learn, and work in whatever way works for them, you make life more accessible to every person.

Reframing traits

I think it's important to use the correct language and say things as they are. A lot of the time when it comes to disability or neurodivergence, able-bodied and neurotypical people try to cover up "negative" terms with ones they are more comfortable with. For example, instead of "disabled" they might say "differently abled." However, this can be very invalidating and ableist, and can be the reason people go undiagnosed or don't get support.

There are also a lot of ways in which neurodivergent people are perceived negatively and given upsetting labels, so I want to offer some alternative language. These terms are not to be used to invalidate difficulties, so I will not be excluding language that identifies aspects that need support. It is for neurodivergent individuals to see another side to the way we get labeled throughout our lives.

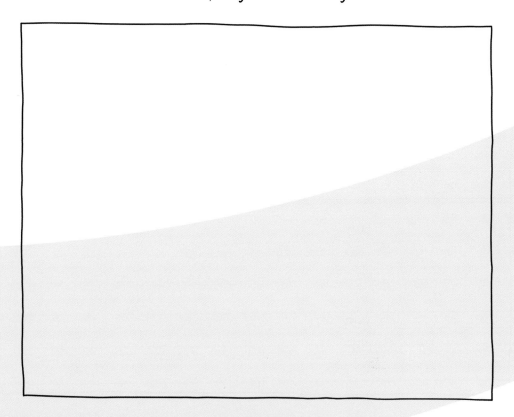

I am:

- ☐ Disruptive
- ☐ Distracting
- ☐ Bubbly
- ☐ Hyperactive
- ☐ Energetic
- ☐ Energizing
- ☐ Passionate
- ☐ Forgetful
- ☐ In-the-moment
- ☐ Present
- ☐ Disorganized
- ☐ Chaotically organized

- ☐ Impulsive
- ☐ Spontaneous
- ☐ Sensitive
- ☐ Emotional
- ☐ Empathetic
- ☐ Sympathetic
- ☐ Enthusiastic
- ☐ Exciting
- ☐ Curious
- ☐ Interesting
- ☐ A problem-solver
- ☐ Adventurous

- ☐ Friendly
- ☐ Outgoing
- ☐ Entertaining
- ☐ Funny
- ☐ Eager
- ☐ Talkative
- ☐ Thoughtful
- ☐ Determined
- ☐ Creative
- ☐
- ☐
- ☐

Acknowledgments

First, I would like to acknowledge that my first book, *I Am Autistic*, has played a large part in the existence of this book. I had never intended on becoming an author, but the feedback I received on the book and the opportunities it has led to — such as speaking at conferences and providing training to teachers — have given me a greater sense of purpose. In particular, it has been a privilege to see the excitement and relief from young, neurodivergent readers who had previously felt alone in many of their experiences. As heartbreaking and overwhelming as some of those interactions can be, they've also helped me to feel less alone myself, more confident, and increasingly reassured that our future generations are open to listening and making more space for differences. I would like to acknowledge Read NZ Te Pou Muramura, as well as Hawke's Bay Readers and Writers Trust, for enabling and supporting some of the opportunities that I've had the privilege of experiencing.

I would specifically like to acknowledge and thank Orla McNeice, Megan McNeice, Ruth Monk, Angela Desmarais, Erin Rayner, and Tayla Alexander-Crawford for reviewing the information in this book. Their experience and expertise come from a range of fields: lived experience as ADHD or AuDHD individuals, experience working with neurodivergent individuals, relevant study and qualifications, and work in the disability and advocacy sectors. Their input was incredibly valuable in ensuring I was producing a work that is respectful, positive and inclusive, and that accurately reflects a wider range of experiences than just my own.

I would like to thank my publishing team at Allen & Unwin. I cannot say thank you enough for the work they have done and the way they've adjusted to working with me. My publisher, Michelle, has always remained supportive, not just with my writing but also with the many other places life takes me. Leanne has done an amazing job of ensuring that everything runs smoothly, taking the extra time to explain things thoroughly to avoid any frustrations or miscommunications. I am grateful to freelancer Sarah Ell for her editing contributions to both of my books so far. And Megan has, again, been wonderful to work with on the design and layout. I also want to acknowledge that the encouragement and support I have received from the team at Allen & Unwin extends beyond the production of the book and involves a number of other people, including Abba, Courtney, Sandra, and Nyssa. Thank you for the patience and understanding you have all shown, and for sharing in my frustration, sadness, hope, and excitement as you get a glimpse of life through my eyes.

Author photograph © Judah Plester

About the author

Chanelle Moriah (they/them) is a neurodivergent author and illustrator who is passionate about creating spaces of understanding to allow the freedom of individual expression. As a late-diagnosed autistic ADHDer, with other related conditions and forms of neurodivergence, they are particularly passionate about bringing awareness to the different ways in which neurodivergence can present, and the importance of being able to live your life accordingly. They hope that by sharing their life and experiences, and helping others to understand, they are reducing the harm and trauma (even if only for one person) that neurodivergent individuals face in existing in a neurotypical world.

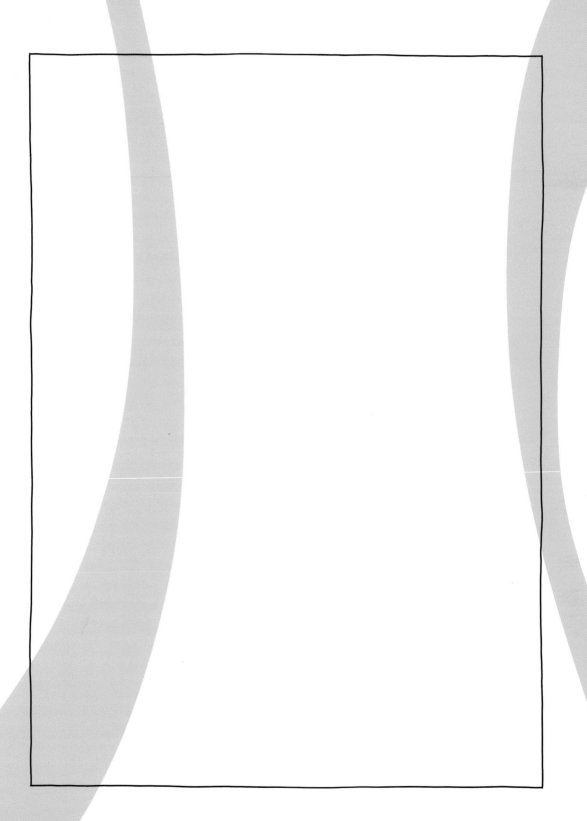